I Am Not Bipolar

I AM TRIPOLAR

A JOURNEY OF SELF-DISCOVERY AND SELF-ACCEPTANCE

Talking about it is not enough

ALLE GONZALEZ

Alle Gonzalez — *Oct. 21/2022*

WOW Book Publishing™

I AM TRIPOLAR.

First edition published by WOW Book Publishing™ and Vishal Morjaria at WowBookPublishing.com

www.IamTRIPOLAR.com

Copyright © 2022 Alexandra Gonzalez

ISBN: 9798849772486

Warning–Disclaimer

Printed and bound in Toronto, Canada

Dedication

Many times, others notice things before we even do so. I appreciated the way my friends raised awareness in me of my own patterns of behaviour. It wasn't easy to accept their feedback. I had to learn to be okay with that without feeling defensive or snapping at others out of pride and shame.

When we are not feeling well, it is so hard to interact with those we love because our mind puts us in a place of disbelief. Many times, the rejection or non-acceptance of our own condition and illness is hard for them to face. I am grateful that I have so many people that care around me.

I am also grateful for my family because they are the most important people in my life, and it is hard to talk with them about these things. I feel as if I have or will disappoint them. Only with time, I understood that accepting my own experiences is actually empowering. Please remind me of this quote when I am having one of my 'bad' days.

If we embark on a journey of self-discovery and self-acceptance, our challenges can be turned into opportunities: our diagnosis into a gift to unravel. Actually, when we learn to self-care, we can channel that energy that seems to be tearing us down into a catalyzer—a force we can generate—that can change the world around us.

What I call being TRIPOLAR is the certainty that anyone is way more than their diagnosis or limitations and way smarter than they think, because in the end, we all can trick our mind into doing great things.

My journey is a journey of self-discovery and self-acceptance.

I hope you can one day journal yours. Be proud of who you are today, what you experienced and who you are becoming. Be proud of being TRIPOLAR.

Contents

Testimonials

"In 2005, I was fortunate to move into a home right beside Alexandra. I was most impressed with her cheerful, upbeat attitude while juggling the demands of her family. Although she was very busy with a newborn and two school-aged children, Alexandra always found time to serve her church and give herself to those who needed her. Over the years she's become a steadfast, supportive friend, who is never too busy to lend a hand when needed. Her positive mindset, easy smile and kind heart make her easy to love. I am grateful to have such a special big-hearted friend in my life."

–KIM L.
London, Ontario

"Alexa is the epitome of a renaissance woman. She has the ability to coordinate her broad range of education, compassion, empathy and motivation to herself and others. Alexa's enthusiasm is contagious as is evident by the amount of yarn I have amassed!!! Alexa encouraged me to crochet as a form of healing. Her supportive reassurance

has led me to make blankets for those who need comfort. Alexa pays it forward."

–NAOMI T.
Mississauga, Ontario

"Alexandra is a very intelligent, energetic and loving lady. She is full of wonderful ideas always geared to help her community, not only in spiritual ways, but also anything related to help us grow and become better human beings. I've been part of Alex's initiatives not only as a participant member, but also donating my time and ideas or knowledge. Alex's initiatives have given me the opportunity to know and belong to a group of like-minded women who have become a very important part of my life! I have learned many different things through the past decade being part of the activities organized by Alex . . . from cooking or being more efficient at the daily tasks of a homemaker to the hardest job of how to be a better parent and wife. I'm grateful for all that Alex has given our local community and me personally as well! I'm a better person because of her generous heart!"

–DINORAH M.
Oakville, Ontario

"I admire Alexa deeply. I consider her a genius and a warrior. Her faith, persistence and resilience have helped her to turn the solitude of her bipolar condition into ART. In the years we have been together as friends, I have seen her overcome battles and turn obstacles into evolution

and development of her professional and personal self. She is an exceptionally kind-hearted and generous woman and an unconditional friend with a sweet and pure heart that inspires other women. Alexa reminds me of Chiron the Centaur in Greek Mythology. During a skirmish with a rowdy bunch of centaurs, Hercules accidentally wounded his friend and mentor, Chiron, in the knee with one of his arrows . . . The arrows Hercules had chosen to use were coated with the blood of the monster Hydra. Arrows coated with the blood of the Hydra were known to cause painful wounds that would never heal. Chiron would never be able to heal from the wound caused by Hercules and being immortal, he could never die. Chiron, a centaur, was known as a wise teacher, healer and prophet. He learns about deep pain and suffering, both in body and soul. Through the acceptance of his own struggles, he becomes The Wounded Healer. He can heal others even if he can't heal himself, condemned to everlasting pain. He could have become embittered or turned it into anger against others, instead, his pain made him wise, taught him about the nature of pain and thus made him the greatest healer in Greek Mythology. For me Alexa is represented in this legend."

–ALEX M.
Canadian Latino Experimental Theatre, Ontario.

"In the time that I have known Alexa I have admired her persistence and her focus. She is the kind of person who puts dreams on paper and fulfills them. She is super *detailed and has a clear sense of organization, planning and development. Also, she is multifaceted, with ideas and dreams that she realizes step by step, and when one transmits one to her, her hands begin to move at a magical speed, transcribing dreams on paper to give them color, a path to follow to become concrete. She is a very charismatic, respectful person, faithful to her dreams and beliefs. I believe that being so active and always helping to achieve goals has helped her condition of being Bipolar to take a back seat. Her love to grow, develop and learn is much stronger. She is a very charismatic human being. It has been a pleasure to meet her and to be able to dream together."*

–VICKY CHIAPPARI,
Mississauga Players Theatre Group, Ontario

About the Author

Alle's vision as a bipolar patient is to help clarify many of the myths and the stigmas surrounding this diagnosis. Using what she calls her TRIPOLAR gift, she presents to all of us a journey of self-discovery and self-acceptance.

Having been raised in Colombia and living in Canada for twenty years, Alle's extensive knowledge and expertise in education and the arts empowered her to dig deeper and document her experiences.

Her inquisitive mind led her on a journey to learn about mental health, especially being bipolar and what the diagnosis entails. Her insights helped her to understand the effects the diagnose had on her as a patient, in her relationships with family and friends and to reflect on which strategies she could use to minimize the effects.

She shares ideas that help create awareness, manage bipolar swings, and overcome the fear of using medication. These strategies have helped her to become productive and keep up with a life worth living. Learning to validate her own condition, she looks at being bipolar as a gift she needs to unravel. In her journey she answered many questions that helped her understand that being bipolar is manageable and one can be functional.

Do you feel that you are not capable or are worth less than others due to being bipolar? Is your life spinning out of control because of being bipolar? Are you looking for a clear understanding of the struggles with anxiety, bipolar and other kinds of mental distress?

This book exemplifies and portrays real situations where you can monitor yourself and act proactively to overcome symptoms, creating a sense of self-worth and self-understanding.

Learn more about Alle at www.IamTRIPOLAR.com

Foreword

It is hard to see all the concepts that I have passed on for years into action. Alexandra is little by little understanding and mastering her WOW. A very particular and interesting title sums up her experiences as a bipolar patient and at the same time a successful and determined professional. I have seen in my WOW Book Camps the determination and the commitment of many to finally come out with a complete book in a short period of time. I am proud to present the foreword of this book.

There are no coincidences in life. Being able to meet on an on-line platform with people around the world is one of the greatest results of this new technological age. There are so many stories to be told and Alexandra sums up her experiences and owns the responsibility for her own life. Like every other person who one day decides to publish a book, she is now able to move further than where she was at the start. She is presenting to us a unique, innovative and clear picture of the challenges that with her commitment and determination will make a mark on her life and in the lives of all who meet her. Everything happens for a reason and I have seen her mature into a determined author that values learning and that is willing to follow advice to reach higher grounds.

I wish her the best in the future, to surround herself with the right people, to keep reaching out and developing those amazing projects. I know that this WOW Book Camp has unleashed a world of possibilities for her. Keep on writing, keep on growing. Alexandra don't forget the bet, because as you have learned, many are able to finish a book in three days.

–VISHAL MORJARIA
International Speaker and Award-Winning Author
MASTER YOUR WOW.
Discover the Real Secret of the Rich.
MasterYourWOW.com
Wowbookpublishing.com

Acknowledgements

First and foremost, I want to acknowledge the land where I was born, the beautiful country of Colombia that has suffered for many years under the yoke of violence and injustice. If I can do one good thing in this world it would be to join forces with my fellow compatriots all over the world and give back by promoting educational programs for the younger generations.

I want to acknowledge the land of Canada, the country I call my home that welcomed my family and me, where I learned the meaning of a just and fair society. Without any doubt my heart is both Canadian and Colombian.

To all the doctors, psychologists, psychiatrists, therapists, friends and family that have walked with me on the journey to discovering this crazy but amazing Bipolar gift—it is because of your expertise, knowledge, patience and support that I am able to be here today.

To my three wonderful kids, all my admiration and my love. They know they are my life, that I am totally and absolutely, madly in love with who they have become and wish for them the protection of God at all times. To Him, the Almighty God of love and mercy, and to no one else goes all the Glory. A Dios toda la Gloria!

Note to the reader

The information, including opinions and analyses, contained herein is based on the author's personal experiences and is not intended to provide professional advice.

The author and the publisher make no warranties, either expressed or implied, concerning the accuracy, applicability, effectiveness, reliability, or suitability of the contents. If you wish to apply or follow the advice or recommendations mentioned herein, you take full responsibility for your actions. The author and publisher of this book shall in no event be held liable for any direct, indirect, incidental, or consequential damages arising directly or indirectly from the use of any of the information contained in this book.

All content is for information only and is not warranted for content accuracy or any other implied or explicit purpose.

My TRIPOLAR mind exists only in English. It is weird but true and I've tried to find the cause. I believe it was my effort, my desire to adapt and to take in every second, every minute of the life I have experienced in Canada, the country I love and call my home. That is also why you will find a few words in Spanish without being translated. I apologize but in my TRIPOLAR mind, and in my heart, I know that what that word expresses to me in Spanish, does not exist in the English language.

Part 1

I AM TRIPOLAR

MY BIPOLAR JOURNEY

1

Who am I?

My name is Alle Gonzalez. I am Colombian by birth and Canadian by choice. I am fifty years old. I am an engineer by profession, an artist and entrepreneur. Why did I decide to write this book? Well, I think it is the sum of many different factors.

First of all, I have become really good with words, especially in English. Though it is my second language, in my bipolar mind it is my first. Let me elaborate on that. I grew up in Colombia and attended a bilingual British school from JK (Kinder) to Grade Eleven. Both elementary and high school (Bachillerato) were at the same location. I practiced my English on a sporadic basis; when we went on vacation while singing all the songs the different radio stations would feature in English. I always got the lyrics wrong. Even today, what my mind thought was said, was not what was really said. I was actually shocked the first time that I played 'Guitar Hero' and I saw the lyrics written on the screen. I was like, "Oh no!!" I never really understood the meaning of many of the songs that I heard growing up in the eighties.

My understanding of lyrics hasn't changed with time. I definitely don't get the lyrics of the songs my children listen to while working out or when we are together in the car. I need to print or at least read them once or twice in order to understand what a song is about and follow. I graduated in Colombia as an Industrial Engineer and worked for ten years in consultancy. Our family moved to Canada after an unfortunate incident where our car was stolen by force, leaving feelings of fear and concern we were not able to live with. We immigrated as independent professionals in 2002. When I started working in Canada, I worked afternoons at the preschool my youngest son was attending. It was an eye-opening experience and the beginning of my career in education.

My journey of twenty years as an immigrant, a woman, a wife, a mother and a friend contrasted with my life as a daughter of Colombian parents. I had the best of both worlds. Because I was always able to go back to Colombia, my children grew up in a Spanish speaking household, educated in English and French. They are a mix of the Latino and Canadian culture. I feel proud to say that I made every effort to understand, learn and adapt to the

Canadian way of life. My best friends are English speaking. I was also active in the Spanish community, especially at my parish where I led a mother's group and catechism classes. It was a safe and comfortable environment for me. I also learned to love winter.

I had a lot of energy and wanted to give back to Canada, the country that became my home. I also desired to give my life a deeper purpose, so I participated actively in parent groups at the school level. As a newcomer, I really appreciated many of the wonderful gifts the Canadian society had available and accessible to everyone. Available meaning you could access them, accessible meaning they were literally in the palm of your hand. If you grew up in a country different from Canada, you would understand why I was so pleased and surprised by the amazing sense of community here. I really mean totally AMAZING. Kids went to school with their neighbour friends. They could walk to school together. In my homeland, we took a bus to drive us across the city, morning and afternoon, back and forth. We had to wake up early in the morning, before six am, and the bus would pick us up and drop us off after three pm, in front of our house. The bus sometimes waited outside the house for us, if we were not ready to go.

Here in Canada, education is publicly funded by the taxes we pay. You just need to register at the school of your choice and a spot is granted to you. It is accessible to every child. This is a completely different from my own

Colombian private education experience: A system where you had to apply to the school of your choice, take an exam and wait to be accepted. Many factors were taken into account to make that decision. In Ontario, the schools provided everything the children needed for schooling: textbooks, paper, crayons, etc. and had a no uniform policy. In Colombia, before the school year started, we received a list of school supplies. We had to try on uniforms and buy everything we needed before the school year started. It was a quite detailed and extensive list. On their first day of school in Canada, my kids carried a water bottle, a lunch bag and a Kleenex box inside their backpacks. That was it. Another thing about Canada was we had to pack them a lunch to eat at school every day. There was a twenty-minute lunch period to eat and children would come home before noon, as kindergarten, at that time, was a half-day program. Everything sounded great: 8:15am to 11:30am and then the kids will be back home for playdates and rest.

I also learned of the incredible programs run at the community centers and the library. This was new for me. I was grateful for the opportunities my children had and I made sure I mentioned that to teachers and administrators who looked at me puzzled. "This is not the way education and communities run in other countries," I said. "This school system is unique to the world." I also appreciated the neighbourhood spirit and the way people greeted, helped and enjoyed one another. That was a huge gift and the neighbours ended up becoming your lifetime friends.

In Colombia, I hardly knew my neighbours. We all were too busy and uninterested in becoming friends.

For us, family was everything. I had the chance to start working afternoons at a Child Care Center in the Before and After School Program, taking care of children. I went to work and stayed in a room with another educator, taking care of the children until their parents picked them up at the end of the day. That was new to me too. In Colombia, children are dropped at home after school by a bus and stay with hired personnel until parents arrive at the end of the day. This was a pretty busy but simple life. Day after day, same routine: wake up, get ready, breakfast, go to school, pick up, lunch, go to work and back home to prepare for the next day.

I had to spice up my life so, with time, we went to every playground, activity, and park, with friends and other moms. We were enjoying life and sharing memories while raising our children. This is where things got a little bit crazy for me. I was such an optimist and made a tremendous effort to adapt, to understand the culture and the language that everything I did, and everything I could read, I did in the two languages. I had the Spanish and English version of each book I was reading and compared them line by line, word by word, in my desire to adapt to my new environment. I cannot prove it, but I believe that was the start of my bipolar condition.

People don't believe me, but I am really shy. I was shy at school and that did not change in university. It is a trait

I've always had and that will stay with me forever. I consider myself an introvert, but life turned around for me and I became a very friendly person who extends sympathy to others. I am not an extrovert. I force myself to come out of my shell, but there is a huge part of me that is just mine which I don't like to share with everyone. Inspired and supported by my parish priest I took a Pastoral Ministry Course at the St. Peter's Seminary in London, Ontario. It was in this course and through the three years of studies that my writing skills in English accelerated. With the help of my beloved neighbour, I started to think and write in English comfortably, leaving behind many of the Spanish language rules that did not apply to the English language.

2

The Effect of the Lockdowns.

My writing career is the effect of the lockdowns. In these last two years of the COVID-19 pandemic, I came to learn more about myself than I had known in my whole life. I dyed my hair blonde since I was fifteen, so when the pandemic hit and hair salons were closed for sixteen weeks, I did not recognize myself in the mirror. I remember that six weeks into the first lockdown, the sales of hair colour products skyrocketed and I realized I did not know what my real, natural hair colour was. I did a wash with a dark ash-brown tone, just to realize, there was not a blonde hair on my head. Worst, I realized that actually, my white hairs (canas) were clearly present and there to stay. This is a very superficial note, as the pandemic was really a catastrophe, a human catastrophe that touched every human being on the planet.

The solitude, distress, anguish and unbearable anticipation of not knowing what to expect during those first weeks of the lockdown, hurt deeply. All over the world we were seeing hundreds of cases of sick people and lives lost to an invisible enemy. There were so many questions with no answers that turned into more questions with no answers. I will never forget the images of hospitals in Italy and Spain those first weeks of March of 2020. I watched a British Newscast on television where the Spanish Health Minister acknowledged their incapacity to protect their elderly. This same incapacity was witnessed in the lives lost in retirement residences in Canada. I am not trying to downplay all the dimensions of this great crisis. I am just putting together some scattered memories of those first weeks. I was by myself at home. I was traveling when the lockdown started and had to come back when the Prime Minister called Canadians to come home because the borders with the USA would be closed.

Flying inside an almost empty airplane felt surreal. I was going to Florida on a mission, with a mask, gloves and a coat that I took off and stored in a plastic garbage bag, before getting into my brother's car. It was insane flying back to Canada, in full PPE (personal protection equipment), and walking through an airport that looked more like a ghost city. They sent me on a direct flight to Toronto and when I arrived, I locked myself in my apartment for two weeks, isolated. I had never before been completely alone in my whole life.

That was the start of my self-discovery and self-restoring journey.

I was diagnosed as a Bipolar II patient in July 2005 after I suffered a manic episode that landed me in the psychiatric ward of the Oakville Trafalgar Hospital. It was the result of a postpartum depression after the birth of my third child. I was lost and unsure of what had happened. It was triggered by a difficult situation. I was devastated. I was saved and taken care of by the love and the goodness of my siblings. Heroically and unexpectedly for me, they drove, flew and arrived at the hospital, looking for me. I had a surreal experience. It was more like an out-of-body experience as I was sedated in the emergency room on an evening and woke up days later in a hospital room, dressed in a white gown, and sleeping in a two-bedroom, side-by-side, with an elderly lady.

My life was never the same after that experience. It was hurtful and I did not understand what had happened. I was not myself. Worse, I had three children, one of them a four-month-old baby that I was breastfeeding and suddenly I did not know where they were. Many years went by before I could talk about it and come to terms with my own experience. It was a real nightmare or in other words, a life-changing experience. The experience was a curveball that life threw at me, but I was willing to receive the curveball and hit back. Life does not always happen as we expect. So many things are out of our sight and out of our control. No matter our disposition to learn and try to understand, there is so much we can't unravel. I needed time to understand the consequences of the bipolar II diagnosis on my life.

Acceptance of the sickness is one thing but understanding what the sickness really is and what it entails is another thing. If we are to be sincere, first of all, we need medical help and support. Then we need to understand and realize that our condition has consequences in our relationships and in our lives. These are the unexpected situations that life throws at us. As one of my doctors said, I am "by far, one of the most functional bipolar patients she knows." I knew that. I did not miss a day of work nor had any other clinical setbacks. My bipolar mind was a hyperactive mind, a smart mind and a flexible mind. I could feel when things were not going well, and I had the chance to take action and keep myself well. That wasn't done by me alone. I was blessed with a close-knit and attentive family, a fantastic group of friends and a support system made up of my family doctor and my psychiatrist that have kept me well over the years. I did have several more depressive and manic episodes; I suffered from SAD syndrome- the Seasonal Affective Disorder—that is a bit more than what we call the "winter blues". Winters are hard. I have to rely on my vitamin D and my sunlamp to be okay. My book is not a book of tragedy though, it is a book of reflection. I hope that through my experiences and through my understanding of this diagnosis and its implications, many families, partners and patients can learn to live in peace with someone who is bipolar or being bipolar.

I AM DETERMINED TO BEAT THE STIGMA OF BIPOLARITY. More and more, we get to know people who are diagnosed with bipolar disorder, depression, anxiety and panic attacks. Without being a doctor, I can say all these conditions are the result of an imbalance in our brain. Medication has been for me, my saving board. I understand how common the rejection of being medicated is. I understand how much we want our bodies to just respond and have this condition under control. I was there once. I asked my psychiatrist to reduce my dose to the minimum possible, I went through cognitive therapy sessions, and I had monthly sessions with my psychiatrist. My family doctor and I check constantly how I am and how I feel, especially since I have turned perimenopausal. Why? Because in the case of women, our moods are also connected to our hormonal changes.

I am not familiar with men diagnosed with bipolar disorder. All I know is that we struggle in the same way with being medicated and being kept under observation, while we find what our bodies need to get settled and tame our minds. We suffer from an invisible sickness that is not completely understood yet by the world. In the early years of my diagnosis, in 2012, while I was visiting Colombia, my mom came across a newspaper article about a book written by the Argentinian clinical psychologist, Eduardo H. Grecco, who is bipolar himself. This article and reading his books brought insights into my life that helped me come to terms with my diagnosis and caused me to be determined to try to keep myself well and stable.

Here is the link to the article: https://www.eltiempo.com/archivo/documento/CMS-12379364—This is the title of the article in Spanish: "La bipolaridad puede esconder un don. Según el psicólogo Eduardo Grecco el bipolar puede tener un talento que no ha logrado desarrollar." This would be my English translation of the title: "Bipolarity can be a hidden gift. According to Psychologist, Eduardo H. Grecco, a person who is bipolar can have a talent that has not yet been developed."

Yes, he nailed it. Dr. Grecco is bipolar himself, and in his two books La bipolaridad como don (Bipolarity as a gift) and Despertar el don bipolar (Discovering or Awakening the Bipolar gift) he taught me how my sickness was not a burden, but a gift to be unraveled. I promise you, that if you stay with me for the next 10 pages, you will not need to read anything else to understand the point I am trying to make. I give total credit to whoever summarized, in that article, the findings of this insightful psychologist called Eduardo H. Grecco. I hope one day I can meet with him in person. I would shake his hand and thank him for the brave and courageous stand he has taken to explain, untangle and bring back to grace what being bipolar is. Thank you!

I have not read that article in a long time. Its essence, I can assure you, has stayed with me forever. I decided that the best way to pass on the message to you is to break down line by line the truths that are stated in that newspaper article. Beyond that, it is up to you, to link it to your own reality and to your own life experiences. I am well aware that the way its content has resonated with me might not be the same way it will resonate with you, and that is okay. We are all at different stages in our journey. I hope these findings set you on the path of a peaceful and rewarding self-discovery and self-restoring journey.

CALLING OURSELVES BIPOLAR IS AN UNDERSTATE-MENT. It is a limiting belief and does not honour the fantastic human beings that we are. We are more than the two moods between which our emotions fluctuate. Ninety percent of the time, if not more, we are functional, regular, "NORMAL" people. There is that percentage of the time, mostly while we are asleep, that our brain keeps functioning, rolling, getting our body exhausted, robbing our energy and leaving us depleted. During this time, we are unable to cope with the world.

It was in that consciousness of the unconscious where I found my peace. Being conscious and aware of what happens in the back of my mind, of the changes we all go through as we raise a family and as we age. In other words, as human beings we are subjected to physical changes that we don't even notice. The biggest changes in my moods were related to my fertile cycle. I never used contraception. I used natural family planning and still dealt with problems of infertility and not being able to maintain pregnancies. The ups and downs of my estrogen and progesterone levels altered my moods and made me susceptible to so many swings, that I could not label my emotions properly.

OUR MOOD SWINGS ARE JUST THAT, SWINGS OF NORMAL EMOTIONS. One of the hardest things to understand about bipolar disorder is that we are not aliens. We are not out of this world or weirdos. Why? Our only issue is that we cannot stop the swinging between emotions. But who can? It is as negative for people to feel excessively than to not be able to feel at all. Many books, articles and medical reviews point to our experience in the womb or to an emotional wound of the past as the cause of the oscillation. For me, at this point, it doesn't really matter. I don't really care why. Now that I have made peace with my own emotionality, the cause is irrelevant.

What is really relevant is how much you are swinging between the emotions of being sad and being happy. How sad are you? How happy are you? How often are those swings happening? Is it daily? Is it weekly? Is it monthly? Is it seasonal? You can map your emotions very easily if you compare them with a child on a swing set. Are you the kid that swings up and down like crazy? The one adults would yell at because we worried they could get hurt? Let's use the law of physics which states that for every action, there is a reaction. If you pull yourself very high, the lows will be very low, and you can lose control of the swing. If you are cautious and find a rhythm that works for you, you will have a pleasant time. Do you see where the dilemma is? It is in how high YOU WANT to swing. For me, being bipolar without the meds is like swinging without any limits.

The use of medication can be a personal decision. It is not as easy as deciding to take a Tylenol for a headache, but as important as using insulin if you are a diabetic or deciding to do chemo if you have cancer. It is at that same level for me. I don't mean to be a pusher, but I believe only time and the methodic, obedient and appropriate use of a prescribed medication brings stability. Once you have gained the confidence in your own self and your body, you can evaluate, talk with your doctor and decide if it works for you. Why am I such an advocate for getting the right medication? Because in one day, my psychiatrist, who I consider a good friend, changed my mood so that I could cope with a difficult situation without hurting myself. I say he is a genius, because he did not switch my medication, which I had been taking for twelve years, but adjusted the dose and opted for the XR version, which is an all-day release. That was it. He also added an antidepressant, and I was hesitant. I did not want to take both medications at the same time. What if they damaged my kidney or liver function? Did I really need them? I struggled for weeks, maybe even months, with these thoughts and it was hard. I was not able to manage two medications. He turned to me and said: "Maria, take them together at night." That worked! My first name is Maria. Only my doctors, my lawyers and any law officers call me by my first name. My friends and coworkers call me Alexa or Alexandra or Alle, so even in the number of names I have, I am TRIPOLAR.

If we know how often the swings are happening and how high the highs are and how low the lows are, we can act upon them. If it is the swinging that disturbs our functionality, then finding a pattern will definitely help us to be proactive and anticipate the moods. Most of us are not used to examining ourselves, so we can't really map the state of our mind. We stay on the surface, making people uncomfortable because we are not okay, and they don't know what to do. We end up losing hope in ourselves. We feel people don't care, but the truth is they care so much that it hurts. They might even get to the point of shutting you down, or ghosting you, as the new generation would say. When we feel uncomfortable with what we don't understand, we either reject it or attack it. Our highs and lows become a power struggle between opinions and points of view.

These swings of emotion have been accurately portrayed in the Disney movie called 'Inside Out.' Here we see how they are a part of everyone's life since adolescence, or I would say since birth. Who has not seen a baby that smiles only to start crying like crazy because of something scary or it was feeding time? This is the description on Wikipedia.org for the movie: "Within the mind of a girl named Riley are the basic emotions that control her actions—Joy, Sadness, Fear, Disgust, and Anger. Her experiences become memories, stored as colored orbs, which are sent into long-term memory each night. Her five most important "core memories" power aspects of her personality take the form of floating islands. Joy acts as the leader, and she and the rest of the emotions try to limit Sadness's influence." That is the plot of the movie and is something that we all experience in real life. We all want to be happy. Only the geniuses at Pixar could explain emotions in such an easy, animated way. Someone in that team might be TRIPOLAR.

Wikipedia continues: "A major aspect of 'Inside Out' is the way emotions and memories are portrayed in the film. The core memories in the film allow Riley to recall previous experiences which control her emotions and can allow 'mental time travel'. In the film, memories are shown as translucent globes that encapsulate its events, with a different hue depending on the mood of each memory." Wow. This is a great explanation of how we travel back and forth between happy and sad memories. Our moods are what lead us to act in fear and anger or to stay put, erring on the side of caution.

This other comment in Wikipedia just opened a new rainbow of possibilities where we accept that we are conditioned by our experiences and that we feel in certain ways, with regard to certain things, because we all have gone through either positive or traumatic experiences. Here it goes: "Another theme was forgetfulness, representing a 'common but unsupported theory leading to a 'permanent loss of information'." My understanding of this last quote is influenced by a book on exercising the power of your memory. We forget things, because they are considered by our unconscious mind as useless OR because they are too painful. Our minds block them in order to protect us.

I love that movie and the fact that it portrays emotions as individual characters. The characters are represented as being pretty alive, as human beings are. Each emotion is A CHARACTER and it is the wrestling between these emotions which determine our moods. Wikipedia explains: "In Joy and Sadness's absence, Anger, Fear, and Disgust are left in control, with disastrous results, distancing Riley from her parents, friends, and hobbies. Because of this, her personality islands gradually crumble and fall into the 'Memory Dump', where memories are forgotten. Finally, Anger inserts an idea into the console, prompting Riley to run away to Minnesota, believing it will restore her happiness."

This movie deserves a whole workshop to analyze the depth of the concepts that describe the human mind and the range of emotions that influence our trains of thought which lead the "headquarters" of our minds in a set direction. I actually did that analysis for a group of parents, and for some of the attendees, my explanations sounded a bit childish. Do you know why? Adult minds lose flexibility or rather, malleability. Googling its meaning, malleability is a noun. "The definition of *malleability, relates to* the quality or state of being malleable such as: a: capability of being shaped or extended by hammering, forging, etc. The malleability of tin b: capability of being influenced or altered by external forces. The malleability of memory . . . is the first reason why autobiographies should be taken with a grain of salt.–Judith Rich Harris"

The minds of children are in permanent development. We say they are like sponges because they can absorb everything. They are absolutely creative, attentive and malleable. We just have to get used to understanding that a child is not an adult in miniature. They are not a reduction of us, and they do not understand why we as parents act in a certain way or react to things that for them are not that important. This is because our knowledge is formed by our experiences. We know things because we have lived through them, experienced them, and reflected on them and that leads us to take action in different ways. That is why something that is pretty easy for me, can be challenging for someone else. That is why, when I mention something to another person, they might feel pressured. All this is because every human being is a world. So, our planet is made up of billions of "walking worlds" interacting with one another.

The collapse of these "worlds" is the result of under-understood emotions and of the mix and probably incompatibility of different trains of thought. Relationships are complicated. Not per se, because a relationship can be explained as the interaction between two people. What makes it complicated is that every person is a whole world. In conversations, a common saying is not to mix pears with apples, right? Well, our relationships are more like a fruit salad. We are a mix of many fruits, some of which, put together with others, do not mesh. For this reason, couple relationships are like a matching game. You either get the right match, or you lose.

It is clear in the Inside Out movie that happiness is not an emotion. It is a place we all want to go. It is the wrestling between joy and sadness that triggers the other emotions. "When Joy finally understands Sadness's purpose: alerting others when Riley is emotionally overwhelmed and needs help" all falls back into place. This is a skeletal summary of the movie and an even more skeletal picture of human emotions. Emotions also depend on the time of year because they are affected by weather. The way we work and we rest also play a part in our emotional stability. I am not a morning person; most of the time I am a night owl, but I function all day long quite effectively. My days are long. I feel I live in a triple-shift: morning, day and night.

All this analysis, trying to write each sentence together and come up with a simple explanation of my understanding of emotions, has made me exhausted. I truly believe that if adults stopped seeing the world only with their grown-up minds, the world would certainly be better. Kids and this new generation of adolescents and young adults, made up of our children, have got a lot of things right. We have to stop feeling offended by their remarks, by their courage to stand up for their ideals—without resorting to violence of course—and start working together on the world they will be inheriting from us in the near future. With this pandemic, it is more and more obvious that the atrocities and problems of the past need to be solved with audacity while trying to maintain a just equilibrium. This is the work of my lifetime: I am determined to beat the stigma of bipolarity. Together we can create awareness and help people to grow their understanding of the mental challenges we all experience at some point in our lives. We have the opportunity to keep growing as a society and turn the turmoil of the reality we have to live into an opportunity. We have the opportunity to turn despair into hope for a better and more understanding society.

3

I am not bipolar.
I am Tripolar.

Both MEN and WOMEN suffer from the stigma of bipolarity. How many have not been diagnosed and go through life thinking they are not worthy, they are not strong, that something is not okay with them, and they cannot understand why? I would say they are many. We might be able to extrapolate that to the rest of the world. Hundreds of people of all ages suffering in silence, not understanding what is happening.

Look at the stages in life from youth to adolescence, the teenage years, young adulthood until we become elders and tell me now if you were the same in each of those stages. If you are quite young and don't know what I am talking about, I will explain with a beautiful example that enlightened my mind the first time I heard it.

My friend was travelling up north on a summer vacation and stopped at this beautiful place where a male artist was working on his art. The art pieces, as I imagine, must have been beautiful because his sensitivity was. They chatted for a bit and then he said: "I have been married five times." Wow, I thought and yikes!!! However, he then added something really special and fantastic. He ended the phrase like this: "I have been married five times, to the same woman." Wow!!! That is real love, and commitment, and intelligence and reality. Yes, we are not the same when we are young and beautiful as when we are not so young, but still as beautiful. Was he talking about the four seasons of life? No, I think he was going beyond that.

In a book on the seasons of life, Gary Chapman states how we all go through our springs and summers, falls and winters. I think in his case he was referring to time, the seasons chronologically. Spring–being born and growing up; summer–the young adult years; fall–our midlife; and winter–the golden years. At least that is what I assume because although I have the book, I have not read it. Why? I haven't read it because I am TRIPOLAR. I get sidetracked between the desire to read it, buying it immediately and never getting enough time to read it.

Also, because I am TRIPOLAR, I read the index and the ending. Yes, I skip through it and then read the book backward. I check the subtitles and get a glimpse, an idea that then stays in my mind. Then my TRIPOLAR mind starts analyzing, unfolding the meaning it has for me, for my life, for my career and for others. Then my TRIPOLAR mind puts it into paper as a chart full of bubbles and arrows and it becomes a complicated but cool mental map that I can use to present my findings to anyone.

I did that, over and over, in a Mother's Group I belonged to at our parish. We picked up a book and we read it together. Those are probably the only books I have read cover to cover, just because week after week, I had to present a synopsis of the chapters to the moms attending, finding ways in which we could relate the concepts written in the book to our own experiences and struggles. It was mostly relating them to struggles because the state of happiness is pretty much simple unless you are pretending and living a fake happiness. That, my dear friends, is the greatest struggle: to live pretending everything is fine, when it is not.

That is another trait of being TRIPOLAR: I look okay, I sound okay, but sometimes I am not okay. My mind and my being IS conflicted, insecure and in doubt. "Where am I going? What am I doing with my life?" The "is" in the last sentence is not a grammar mistake. Because my mind and my being are one, singular. My mind can be my greatest fan, encouraging me to be courageous and act, but will be putting me down at the first obstacle. The gift of the TRIPOLAR is that instead of letting the mind win a battle, you struggle with it until you master it and tone it down. Prayer, meditation, breathing slowly, and mindfulness are key to taming the mind. Here is another trait of a TRIPOLAR person. I am not only body and spirit. I have a freaking mouth and it functions on its own.

Yes, another of my characteristic TRIPOLAR traits is I cannot keep my mouth shut. I am getting better, or at least I try to keep it shut, but it overpowers my mind and my will. I am weak. In the spring of my life, I guess I wasn't that shy in my family setting because my voice was strong. When I spoke, I definitely set some criteria. I had a mindset and a very clear and inflexible idea of right and wrong. I moved between the light and the darkness, between what was right and what was not, according to me. I held a monochromatic view in black and white, and nothing more than black or white. I probably kept that view over my teen years, during my years at university and during my first years in the workplace. When I came to Canada, my mind discovered the world is not only black and white. There are different shades and mixtures of colours. I discovered how black and white are actually the absorption of all colours or the reflection of all colours.

That discovery made my life move between different shades, between light grays and darker greys. It was only when pain hit my almost-perfect life that I started seeing the world in its full spectrum of colour. It was through suffering deeply, that my eyes could see the interaction of colours in the world around me. I don't mean this literally. I was not colour blind. When you are colour blind, you might not be interested in looking at the world with different eyes. It is like when you unplugged the green cable from the back of the TV, the one that was with the other red and yellow cables, bringing full colour from your antenna port to your television. That was an older system before the new generation of USB and HDMI cables. If you are not familiar with that at all, you can Google it.

Old televisions did not have flat screens and they had a three-headed cable which determined the colours of the image. They were connected to the back of the TV. If you missed connecting one, you would cancel some colour for the image on the screen. If you did not connect the red, your screen would look like different shades of sandy colours. This is the way that colour blind eyes see the world. When the green and red rods are not doing their function, then the world of blues and purples, oranges and reds are blurred away. They can differentiate the colours, of course, but not like we do, in their full spectrum. This was happening to me, limiting my view of reality.

It is hard to be smart, gifted and to learn how to put feelings and sensations into words. I am not labeling but expanding their meaning which is one of the great gifts of my TRIPOLAR mind. What we experience makes us feel a certain way. The way we feel, generates a response. If you are kind, people might be kind to you- not always though, because some people have cold hearts. If you are tough, people will get defensive with you, and they may even feel hurt. In extreme cases, they can even go to the point of experiencing trauma. Six months ago, I did not know this. I took an online course on how to manage trauma in children, and what an eye-opener it was. What is traumatic for me, might not be traumatic for another person and vice versa. People are not weak, they are different, and here is where my mind had an AHA! moment.

Yes, people are not weak, they don't have weak personalities. That concept is a bias that many of us, who are quite strong minded–TRIPOLAR–can use to define other people. So, if you think tripolar is not you, because you are soft, docile, understanding, slow to fight, I am telling you: You might still be Tripolar, but on the opposite side of the spectrum. Like a diamond that we can split in two triangles, one on the top, pointing up, and one on the bottom pointing down. This has been a huge lesson in my life experience. Guess what? The person that refuses to get into a fight is as strong-willed as the person who gets into the fight. It is not a matter of force. It is a matter of temperance. TEMPERANCE is the basis to understanding and dealing with a TRIPOLAR mind.

We don't talk about temperance anymore. Here comes Google again: "Temperance noun -1: moderation in action, thought, or feeling: restraint. 2a: habitual moderation in the indulgence of the appetites or passions. b: moderation in or abstinence from the use of alcoholic beverages."

For this reason, is why going on a diet, adhering to an exercise routine, and even keeping a bedtime and sleep schedule is such a struggle for many of us. Our mind overpowers our will, whether we want it or not. These are a few of the struggles I've had to face, and I know there are many more people who have been diagnosed (or people who know someone who has been diagnosed) that face these same struggles. We are way too ignorant of the capacity of our own minds. Measuring all minds with the same gauge creates a distortion of our own reality as human beings.

Talking about it is not enough. I want to put all my TRIPOLAR principles into action. I want to uplift you, no matter where you are at. Whatever you do is amazing, if it is done with integrity, honour and a rectitude of intention, while looking for the common good. We are here to help. If your motives are dark, selfish, with the wrong agenda in mind and looking to divide, question and attack, life will take its own course and will break you down. The law of karma will take action because what goes around comes around. I don't mean to be mean, but realistic. We as humans have a dark side. 'Star Wars' is not just a movie. It is a full biblical and principle-based philosophy. My TRIPOLAR mind has also sat down with me and analyzed the roles of the Jedi, the Force, Anakin, Obi-wan Kenobi, Darth Vader's fall from grace and the relationship with Padme. This could be more than just a series that gives millions to Disney, MGM and the great networks. If only we could re-focus entertainment into education with a purpose other than just becoming rich and powerful.

4

Why Tripolar? This is my story.

The title for this book came about in June 2021. As I was "finding myself" in the third lockdown. Truly, I really mean finding myself because yes, I was lost. I was lost inside of me. My life had changed. As I often referred to it, my life was changed for me. I had to learn and adapt.

I was hoping to go back to work at least for a few weeks before the end of the school year. I missed the kids, needed to go check my space, wanted to check what we had available for the programs I was running and was looking for a bit of normality after being laid-off work for more than six weeks. Well, that did not happen. The decision was made that schools would not go back in person until September 2021, to allow the chance for more people to get vaccinated and offer a safer space for the children, teachers, administrators and at the end of the day for the families and the community at large. That was disappointing.

That same week, my friend Alex Montealegre, my Colombian twin-sister of different parents, sent me a link to a free book writing webinar called "The 5-day virtual WOW Book Camp". It was free and I was free. I thought, "when at the end, they try to sell me something, I will say no." I am glad I did not let my fears and insecurities stop me at that point. I would have missed the amazing experience of writing this book, of maturing my understanding of my own condition, of my diagnosis as I prefer to call it. I would also have missed the opportunity of meeting amazing people from all over the world that like me, had a toad in our throats, a book to be written. We had a body and a mind full of ideas and experiences stuck inside. I want to honour the knowledge I received and also the way in which my leap of faith, by signing on for that virtual Book Camp, turned into a leap of knowledge that took me straight into the reality of being able to write what I had inside of me.

Tripolar is the way I would love people to call and relate to people like me. The ones that have been diagnosed, judged, and marginalized because of our ignorance. Please if you read this, practice with me: Are you bipolar? "No, I am not bipolar, I am TRIPOLAR. I have a gift that you can't even imagine, and I am unraveling it."

It really sounds weird, but also sounds cool. Be proud of your state of mind. No matter where you are at; in depression, in a panic attack, suffering from anxiety or loneliness. You are not your sufferings. You are going through it. You are on the highway to recovery. Are you depressed? We will be working on getting you better. The first step, and I will never stop saying this, is to please go and reach out to your doctor. It is harder than you can imagine going by yourself to a hospital, a family doctor, or a walk-in clinic saying, "I am bipolar, I am having a depressive episode and I need help". I went through that. It is horrible.

I went to my hometown hospital, on a January night in 2018, four years ago. The Winter Olympics were taking place and I actually missed the bobsledding because I could not wait anymore to get help for the clinical depression I was experiencing. My sister went with me, and the emergency room was packed. After two hours, I went into the triage and stated what I wrote in the previous paragraph: "I am bipolar, I am having a depressive episode and I need help." The nurse turned to me and said, "What is it exactly that is bothering you?" I felt hopeless and defeated realizing a healthcare professional did not understand my pain. It was not physical pain. It was emotional and was hurting as bad as a broken bone. I was put, of course, last on the list. My emergency was not really an emergency in the triage eyes. After three more hours of waiting, no seats available, and a room packed with probably thirty-six people before me, I left. I just had to say, "I am leaving." I also had to sign a paper stating that I was going away. The truth is, staying there was more painful and harmful. My spirit was broken.

I sent a letter to the hospital, saying how disheartening that was. I got a very polite and thoughtful answer from which I understood that on the list of medical priorities, mental health was at the bottom of the list. I got on a phone-list for therapy and also on a program of which I can't remember the name, where someone who had experienced something similar, would call me on the phone. This phone buddy system was great, reassuring and supportive. I looked forward to our monthly conversations. The first professional they assigned me as a therapist on the phone did not work for me. When I mentioned I could not wake up and get up from my bed, the therapist asked me to rely on my willpower and sent me by email some sheets that, if I had not tried to implement over and over, I may have believed they would help. It was all theoretical, like what a manual would suggest in this situation. The manual was right for a robot. All this, I had to deal with on my own. The hardest thing about the bipolar condition is that those who live with you cannot help you. They are too close, too emotionally involved and they cannot handle being with you when you are in this state. This is a sad and crude reality.

My household was a busy home where real people lived. We also had pets, a fish and two dogs. The dogs were always there for me, wagging their tails which meant the world to me. Once I could get myself out of bed, I could move on to doing things. Years later, my son mentioned how hard it was for him to see me lying in bed eighty percent of the time. It must have been difficult to see where I was at, and I understood that was the reason why they could not help me. After my experience with the phone therapist, I resorted to the web. The names are blurry, but the pictures of my life at that time are imprinted in my brain. I found this guy who had walked the way. He had several depressive and suicidal episodes. I would listen to his podcast while I was folding clothes. Yes, once I got out of bed, I was able to cook, clean, wash, drive and work. It was the night that ate at me.

My mom was my rock. When I reached out to her in despair, she made me realize how much they needed me to be well. I felt I had a ticking bomb inside my head. I could not wait for the unconscious part of my brain to stop. The thoughts that took over my being during the night made me wake up exhausted and unable to stand up. I feared for the day that my frontal cortex would be beaten. The moment where my subconscious would overpower my reasoning and my will and I would end up doing things that I did not believe in. I understood, at that moment, where the self-harming and sadly, suicidal thoughts abide and where they would sink into a bipolar mind. I understood what could happen to me if I did not do something about it.

Anatomically, for me, my bipolar state is at the back of my head, close to the neck. I am not sure how I came to this realization, but it is true. In my observations of my behaviours and patterns, I could feel what part of my brain was taking over. It is like those cartoons where you have the little angel talking to you on one side and the little devil talking to you on the other. This illustration was a typical feature of the Disney, Mickey Mouse old cartoons. Whether it was Donald Duck, Pluto or Goofy, they all had these two antagonist characters playing opposing roles and blurring their decisions. They were living proof of the bipolarity inside all of us. Those inside voices either brought you up or tore you down. Whether you listen to one or to the other is a conscious act.

It is confusing. The part of me that was depressed was always at the back of my head and stayed awake while I was sleeping. What was the really weird part was that for a long time I didn't realize the way in which my brain stayed active during the night. I went to bed okay and tired, and my meds would allow me to get a good night's sleep. It was on a December day, when I opened my eyes, that I understood the monster I was battling. The monster was inside my head. It was not me. At that moment, every single podcast I had heard and every bit of knowledge I had gathered about my diagnosis and my condition, fell into place.

5

Leaning on Others

If you are experiencing any type of deep emotion, fear, despair caused by depression, anxiety, going through a bipolar manic episode or a depressive one, please stop here. Take a deep breath and know I am here for you and would like to help. This is the moment where you need to seek medical help. I want to make sure none of you are placed in a situation that can at some point trigger an unconscious response.

I have been able to get to this point because I have been successfully and effectively medicated. After my depressive experience, I took myself to the emergency room at the Credit Valley Hospital in Mississauga. That was it. I could not wait anymore. I had to go and find the right person who could help because up to that point, no one around had been capable to do it. The doctor that I met not only helped me but also saved my life. He put me back together in a day. He listened, he cared. The people that received me at that hospital that day, through the triage, in the emergency room, from the moment that I got in, until I came out with a psychiatrist's prescription, are heroes to me. They might never remember who I was, but I will never forget the kindness they showed me. It was not an easy process. Seven hours of waiting, while I was emotionally destroyed. I was alone. I just had my mom and my sister on the phone.

Please understand there is hope. There is a light at the end of the tunnel. You are here because you are meant to be here. It is not by chance. You were meant to be here in this moment of time, and we need you here. I know this doctor saved my life because one day later, my life changed. Had I not been on the right medication, I don't know what my reaction would have been when my life was torn upside down. That was the power of the medication. It balances my imbalance so that I can cope with the world.

There are things that need to be said. Others, that by not being said, have more meaning. You don't need to, if you don't want to, elaborate on what is happening to you. You don't need to, if you don't want to, share private details of your life. However, you owe to yourself the chance to be okay. Nothing is more valuable than you, no matter what your life is like or the circumstances you are going through. Please open your ears and heart. I care, and I am here to help.

There are institutions that educate in suicide prevention, and we can all learn more about that. Sadly, mental health outcomes are often tragic. The real tragedy is that we notice the obvious too late, once a life has been lost. This might sound like a riddle. The tragedy is not being prepared to do something. The tragedy is not noticing the signs. The tragedy is that suicide is a permanent "solution" to a temporary problem. There is no way back. It is actually not a solution, but a desperate and avoidable mistake made in an attempt to alleviate the pain. It is forgetting there is hope, there is help and light at the end of every tunnel.

We are starting a process of education to beat the stigma. There are many institutions like www.livingworks. net that have it all together. I was not aware of all this information until I started writing these lines. Sometimes when I start writing I do not know where it is taking me and why it ties up with my own story. Let's make this organization known. The wheel has already been invented for more than thirty-five years. I hope this plea guides you and educates you, so you can educate others and we can start breaking the stigma of mental illnesses and start being open about the hurt we all live with.

I am putting in these pages the knowledge I received when I was trained by LIVING WORKS Education on suicide prevention. This is what their brochure safeTALK Resource book and workshop states:

"My open, direct and honest TALK about suicide will make a difference. If many others in my

community TALK about suicide, there is more hope
for my family and my friends -and even me–to be
kept safe from suicide. A community that can TALK
about suicide can TALK about all kinds of things."

"I like this or that" "I care about you" "I need this"
"I enjoy life" THIS IS LifeTALK, another expression
of a suicide-safer community.

I did not realize the importance of that message until a tragedy happened. A boy, probably 16 years old, made an irreversible decision about a school problem. This changed his community and his family forever. The grief of losing even one life by suicide is unbearable for friends and family, and for society as a whole. We never recover from a death by suicide.

I am being very mindful of the language that I use because words and images TRIGGER reactions. My co-worker attended the same suicide prevention workshop that I did. Guess what the difference was. She was not at her best. She was battling a lot of problems that included family, drugs and instability. The workshop triggered so much pain in her. Though the presenters said, "if you experience any triggers, you can leave," it is a rollercoaster of emotions to talk about this, especially if you are vulnerable.

I am one hundred percent sure that as I found help, you can find help too. My great friend once told me the following, and I want to pass it on to you because this was what made me understand how important I was for my own recovery. These were her words: "Your mental health cannot depend on your husband or your kids or your family. Your mental health depends only on you, and it is your own responsibility." What an impact those words had on my life and on my outlook for the future. I have to be my best friend and my best advocate. I have to learn and relearn how to call things by their names, and mainly I have to beat the sickness with my own mind and willpower.

Those who helped me always trusted me. They trusted I was going to do what I needed to do, to be okay for my kids, for my family and for myself. When my life changed, I was confused. I understood in some way how my life was affected by the consequences of my ignorance and incapacity to understand the changes my body was undergoing as I started to age. My body at thirty was not the same as it was at forty, just as it is not the same today, at fifty. It will sound funny, but I think that it is necessary to add some humour to be able to understand the depth of this reality. People had warned me of the aging process. Both of us, male and female age at a different pace. There are all sorts of genetic and diet-related factors, health conditions and even the environment, that affect us, but reaching menopause for women is a totally different reality than what the midlife crisis is for men.

When I arrived in Canada in my thirties, I came to know many other moms. Many of them were at least ten years older than me. Their youngest children were classmates of my kids. I married at twenty-four, while the average

Canadian got married after the age of thirty-two. During a playground conversation, they mentioned that "at forty everything falls down." I had no idea what they were talking about, but I discovered it right when I hit my fourth decade. The day after you get to the 4th floor you start seeing that is exactly what happens. The fact that your skin, everywhere, starts "dropping" is a reality. I was okay with that. A few years later at work, in a kitchen conversation while making snacks, someone spoiled for me the reality of fifty. I was informed that at fifty I would take the shape of a Lego block, with no waistlines. Essentially, I would resemble a trunk. Not that the aging process scared me, it was more that my mind was trying to understand how the heck that happens. Trying to untie these aging knots was the work of my TRIpolar mind.

I quickly realized this process of going from the beauty of the thirties to the challenges of the forties and fifties was directly linked to my hormonal changes as a woman. I am not sure men go through any "hormonal" changes, but sadly, they do change too. Someone once told me: "Men marry hoping their wives will not change, but they do. Women marry hoping their husbands will change, but they don't." This is a crude reality, but also a reality of choice. If you have a mental illness or any kind of illness, for sure changes will happen faster and be more noticeable. The woman will mostly be referred to as crazy. It is a very sad reality but in most cases true.

It is quite unfair, but true. We still live in a male-oriented society. Women have a huge responsibility for raising the children, maintaining the house, keeping up with social relations and we are expected to become income earners too. There is a lot of pressure on our shoulders, and we try to manage it as best as we can, only to realize our bodies at some point break down. We succumb to the pressures of these modern times. Mental illness breaks down families. It causes an imbalance and a struggle that if you cannot deal with it together, has catastrophic consequences. Mental illness makes us more susceptible to the physical changes our bodies go through with the passing of time, to our hormonal changes and to who we are in all our relationships. The hardest part is the family repercussions mental health has. It can affect people, separate parents and siblings, breakdown families with divorce and separation becoming more prominent every day. Adapting our minds and our bodies to the physical and emotional changes brought by our mental challenges is hard. Many times, to survive all we have to do is let go of the bad, change our way of looking at ourselves and appreciate the good.

When you forgive yourself, you don't change the past, you start looking at it with a clear lens. You accept that you were limited in your knowledge and understanding, that having good intentions does not always work. You realize that often, trying to please others and trying to put them first is part of the problem. Where does the idea of being a gift for each other remain? Have we made our relationships something disposable too, like the paper plates and paper cups that save us so much hassle?

This is why it is so hard when we are diagnosed with a mental illness. We stop looking at ourselves with compassion, but with regret. It might not apply to all cases, but it is my case. What did I do to get here? I was never perceived by people the same way again. For my family, I was a fighter, a leader and a survivor. For others I felt I was an inconvenience, a hassle and a burden. My close friends saw me as their soulmate, and they supported me in times of crisis. We cared for and relied on one another. At work I was and continue to be professional and effective. In art, I am and have always been creative and innovative. Strangers have asked themselves: Who is that? I walk with confidence. I speak with some criteria. Many times, I feel I am intimidating, and people stop being natural around me. I try to live with a purpose and live like a normal human being. When people found out I was bipolar, their reaction was "Wow, you don't look like . . .". I wonder, then, how does a bipolar person look to others? Could it be that we appear rushed, busy or temperamental? All of this can be true. My common trait has been that I care too much and that I never stop caring.

Here is where I started trusting again. Because people appreciated me, I made strong bonds. Over time, I can say that I have been blessed with many friendships—not only acquaintances but real friendships. These are not day-to-day friendships, but the kind where no matter how far apart you live and how many years have gone by since you have been in contact, they know that you care. It is unbelievable how I have come in contact with people I had not seen for years and still felt we could connect, at a different level of course. We are different from who we were then. Those friendships are solid. Memories flashback as we start talking and that really lightens our hearts. I guess at the end, when we are fifty, we all know the essence of who we are and who we are not. We give ourselves permission to restore and recover the relationships we had. This applies to both men and women. Human relationships are so complicated because loving another person exactly for who they really are, is a decision we need to make every single day, even on the bad days.

Why is this important when I talk about leaning on others? Well, because love is fragile. It is like peace, there are so many external factors that can alter it. When you are not well, you try to rely on the people closest to you. Only unconditional love survives these challenges. This is a love where you—without being naive—put the other at the same level as you put yourself. Many relationships break because they reach a point of internal criticism and lack of understanding of what we go through. People move away from each other at some point. I hope we realize that every personal choice we make alters other people's lives. As human beings we need to own it, accept the consequences of our decisions and stand behind our own choices, instead of blaming others.

Why is it important to own it? Because when we suffer a loss—call it a relationship, losing a job, feel down by a sickness, have broken ideals or dreams—we tend to blame ourselves and that takes us into a self-destructive path that affects our mental health. "I was not good enough. I did not do enough. I cannot move forward. Was I a failure as a human being? Did I give my best? Is it really my fault?" Relationships are not just social institutions. They are interactions and bonds between people wanting to live and thrive together. This is a day-to-day decision to be together, based not on how I want the other person to be, but based on who the other person really is, with their strengths and struggles. This brought me peace and helped me to understand the complexity of human relations. I understood that inside of us, as human beings, we know who we are and what we stand for. If we have to change the essence of who we are to be with someone, we are not accepting ourselves. It would be like living a lie day after day.

I am not sure if this is useful to others. It was useful to me. I started loving myself again. I am way more than my mistakes—which are many. I am way more than the things I've had to go through in my life. No life is easy. We all have our own degree of "difficulty." We all live in different circumstances, and in the end, no one else can live your life. It took me more than three years to come to terms with that. The thing is, when I did not feel judged and condemned all of the time, I started feeling better. With the help of my amazing doctors (my family doctor, my psychiatrist, the walk-in-clinic doctors and other practitioners I've met in the last years) and the regular, constant and reliable use of my medication, I have come a long way. Pain only makes you stronger. Your character is forged with pain. Being still absolutely imperfect, freaking out more often than not, and having to struggle in my relationships, I have come to realize that my life is an adventure worth living. If I had refused to go through the painful situations of my life, avoiding them or simply by giving in and making the "changes" that people wanted me to make, I would not be here writing these words today.

Lean on others. Trust them. Make sure they love you unconditionally, not only when it is easy, or when it makes sense for them. It is worth living your life by being you. You are bigger than your shortcomings. You are bigger than any diagnosis and you are bigger than your regrets. When you don't have to stop being yourself to be with someone, there is your heaven. Don't look for you outside of yourself, look for your inner self. It is that voice that is with you when you are alone, when no one else is around, and especially that voice that should not change when you are around others. The saying "fake it till you make it," only works partially. You can't fake being yourself. Sometimes we might not like what we see and that's okay, because we have a mind, an intellect and a conscience that tells us when we are obnoxious, selfish and when we are wrong.

That little voice can be tamed. It can be distracted. We can change our patterns of destructive behaviour. All we need is to see them as destructive. If we surround ourselves with things that are not good for us—be it people, food, drink, drugs or even inanimate objects—we end up falling for them, no matter how much we try not to. The saying "don't buy what you don't need" is true in the literal meaning of the phrase. We just add our whims to our needs. We justify our desires to get what we want, independently of the harm they can do to us. Here, I am talking about extremes. Some things might be neutral. When we start living only for the things that make us feel good, we deceive ourselves. Then, when difficulty comes, when something we don't like or something we did not expect falls into our lives, we crash. We can't handle it. I will never forget the phrase from this beautiful and amazing woman dressed in jeans and a white t-shirt on 'America's Got Talent.' Her name was Jane Marczweski. She was a thirty-year-old vocalist who called herself Nightbirde. When Howie said, "nobody would ever know" she was dealing with cancer, Nightbirde replied, "Thank you. It's important that everyone knows that I'm so much more than the bad things that happen to me. You can't wait until life isn't hard anymore before you decide to be happy." She won the hearts of everyone who would ever listen to her voice and her thoughts.

I wonder where and how she came up with such a deep realization. For when she did, she became brave and moved forward to fulfill her dreams. She left all of the viewers speechless and in tears. She got it right and her life now has a meaning millions of times more powerful than before she did that. Can you see the power of being oneself? When I am alone, I stop leaning on others to start leaning on me.

6
Leaning on Me.

Who has inspired me? Wow, so many people have had to fight the good fight. For me, the good fight has meant keeping the faith, especially my faith in humanity after the setbacks that life has thrown at me. I've had to learn to ease my mind. In 2017, I found myself experiencing SAD syndrome again, the Seasonal Affective Disorder. Why? Well, because here in the northern hemisphere, up in North America, winter is quite long. Let's be honest, out of twelve months, six have bitter cold. For years and years, I was told to use a sun lamp. Do you think I did it? No, not until the past three years. Why? Because like everyone else, I am stubborn. We know better. We think we know everything. These last three winters when I intentionally, deliberately placed my lamp in the bathroom and used it from October to May have been a breeze. Yes, I have to accept that part of my imbalance came as a result of not being consistent and not following advice. I was leaning on others to get well rather than leaning on me.

When you start trusting yourself, because no one knows you better than you, you move from feeling like a victim to becoming your own leader. How does this happen? Well, part of it is trusting yourself and part of it comes from experience. My friend was diagnosed with bipolar disorder, like me. Guess what? We could organize a party in a day, actually in only a few hours because we had that gift. The gifts that Dr. Eduardo H. Grecco mentions in his books are a creative capacity, lateral thinking, problem solving, active imagination, intuition, empathy in human relations and emotional intelligence. We think in images. We are extremely curious and want to learn everything. We have a holistic vision. We are resourceful and cope well with adversity. We have the ability to reconcile irreconcilable ideas and concepts. If we are so great, why do we struggle? Well, we are not two peas in a pod.

This is what we are: we are UNIQUE TRIPOLAR beings. A tripod holds your camera stable so that your pictures, photographs and your masterpieces turn out great. This is the idea behind recognizing our TRIPOLAR mind. We need to stop thinking that bipolarity means incompetence and instability. How can we benefit from being bipolar? Well, first of all, take a look at the bipolar gifts. My explanations are easy, and I will refer to them as "Bipolar Gifts for Dummies."

Our creative capacity makes us innovative and yes, creative. New things come out of our minds. Having lateral thinking, we can make connections that lead us to great problem-solving skills. An active imagination, when contained for the good, makes us writers, actors and artists, enriching our life and our communities. Our intuition helps us to detect needs and be proactive. We see things that others don't see yet. This deep empathy in human relations makes us great friends. Our emotional intelligence is a two-way road. We find where other people are, both emotionally and physically, then we detect where we are. We determine the ways in which we can help.

We really try to cope well with adversity by adapting. We have this capacity to associate ideas and concepts that seem irreconcilable and make them one heck of a great plan or project, even a gardening project. We have this extreme curiosity—well intended of course—and become extremely resourceful. We look at the world integrally, as one, and hold a holistic vision which can be defined in psychology as "an approach to understanding the human mind and behaviour that focuses on looking at things as a whole. It is often contrasted with reductionism, which instead tries to break things down into their smallest parts." Does this mean that we add up the sum of all parts and then act upon it? Because if this is so, we are awesome.

These were my new discoveries with Vishal and the WOW book camp. As I started writing, all things fell into place. Not in the linear way in which we think ideas should flow, but in the messy flow of my ups and downs, in the creative thinking oriented by a purpose. It was the way in which this book started to take form. What I thought I was going to write has nothing to do with what I have written.

There has been a lot of learning from watching my children grow up and become young adults. At some point when it started to happen, I had to let go and be more of a spectator than the protagonist of their lives. As they moved away, I realized that my "mom's world" was changing in the way my own mom's words explained it to me. You start doing things for them, then you do things with them so one day, they can do things on their own. "Primero se hacen cosas por ellos, después con ellos para que un día puedan hacerlo solos. Un Hijo no es una extension de tu vida. Los hijos son prestados." A child is not an extension of your life. They are lent to you, for a short period of time. We try to be the best parents we can with the resources that we have. We try to hold everything together in our hearts and everything in our hands, but two hands are not enough. We need a village to raise a child. There are more than forty developmental assets that help children become great human beings. We will love our children with all our hearts, regardless of who they become. The first five years of life are the most important. This is the base of pedagogy and the focus in education that we are passing on to the next generation.

Our children are given to us on loan. This is probably the most precious loan you will ever receive and one that life makes sure you pay back. I hope when my kids have their own children and are as old as me, they realize they grew up as very happy kids. I was a happy child, sometimes bad tempered and a bit spoiled, yet happy. It is important to have an overall view of our lives. A bird's eye view, so we can detect when our problems arise and what happens with our bodies as we age. Then, we will be able to come to terms with our own lives and do good in the world. Why? As I said before, you being here is not by chance. You were meant to live in this moment of time, and we need you here.

We are who we are. We just need to keep our eyes on the final goal and do what it takes to get there. We don't start with big things like skyscrapers. We start one brick at a time and before we place those bricks, we need to do a lot of digging. We will need to dig inside ourselves as it is done at any great construction site. How high you are able to build is correlated to how deep you have to dig before. <u>Because our measure in life is exactly the same measure of what we have inside of us.</u>

I am not a civil engineer, but my understanding is that the amount of soil you have to excavate and remove from a site must match the exact weight of the building put up on that site. This balance is what will make your building or project not only feasible but safe. Does this make sense? If not, I have just come up with a new concept created by my TRIPOLAR mind.

7

How to be Functional.

It is up to you whether you want to go high or stay low, whether you want to shine or be dull. All of this is okay, we are all different. The thing we will have in common is the desire to be okay, to be understood and to be able to live a happy and valuable life. My ideas have been put into action with this book and the help of all the people around me who care enough to see me well.

Read this poem with me. The Peace Prayer by St. Francis of Assisi.

"Lord, make me an instrument of Thy peace;
Where there is hatred, let me sow love;
Where there is injury, pardon;
Where there is error, the truth;

Where there is doubt, faith;
Where there is despair, hope;
Where there is darkness, light;
And where there is sadness, joy.

O Divine Master,
Grant that I may not so much seek
To be consoled, as to console;
To be understood, as to understand;
To be loved as to love.

For it is in giving that we receive;
It is in pardoning that we are pardoned;
And it is in dying that we are born to eternal life."

This poem is in the public domain. It reflects spirituality. Yes. Is it only for a certain group of people? No, I don't think so. Even the worst people love something. Parents would never give a snake to their children instead of bread because hurting others on purpose is pathological.

We do ride on an emotional rollercoaster. On one of my summer vacations in Florida, where for many years my family met to spend time together with the grandparents, aunts, uncles and cousins, I got a beautiful notepad. I got it mostly because it was colourful and had an amazing picture on the front that said: "When Life Becomes a Roller Coaster, Climb into the Front Seat, Throw Your Arms in the Air, & Enjoy The Ride!". It was not a regular pad. It was a notepad that amazed my TRIPOLAR mind. Suzy Toronto . . . feel the tingle, is the author. The black and white linear pattern that encompassed the cover of the pad caught my sight. The glitter in the green, small carts of the rollercoaster and in the bracelet and head barrette was gorgeous. The long red hair with mustard highlights flying gave a sense of movement. The hands in the air, plus the dark shades that highlighted her face told me she really was enjoying the ride. You don't just come up with a saying like that. You must have thought a lot on how to give that meaning to an image. I love it. I have used it only for very special notes. Sometimes the best thing about getting beautiful things that inspire you is having them, because of the way they make you feel.

I need to say this because if I didn't, I could not go on explaining how we need to label and round up our emotions. One set of emotions for men: I am happy, can mean 225 different things for a woman. It can be "I am so happy for you," or "See that baby? That makes me so happy," or "Happy Birthday!" When we are happy, we are not just happy. We feel excited, motivated, energetic, delighted and amused. We can also feel supportive, daring, recognized, creative and free to feel. We can also be going through an exciting, sexy and playful moment. When we are sad, we feel miserable, depressed and many times even guilty for not being okay. We may get sleepy, would like to be alone, get bored, feel inadequate or apathetic to what happens around us. Sadness breaks our balance. We feel defeated because we think we should always be okay. Can't a mom have a bad day? Not without scheduling it. "Hey honey, tomorrow I will be sad, please get ready for that ride." No, that does not happen in real life.

Some situations make us switch from sad to happy, because our bodies that have that beautiful possibility of generating life, lose their equilibrium in many ways. If you are a mother, have you realized that for every pregnancy, a whole human being with all the functions to be alive, grew inside your body? You have sustained each one of your children in their growth for approximately nine months inside of you, sharing all the functions of your organs, and all this, while moving around, having a life, developing a career, raising a family, and yes taking care of other adults around you. Tell me of a system inside a lab that can beat this. I would love to see it working. And, if it works, please let me know if that same pattern can be repeated millions of times in all parts of the world, for centuries, in different circumstances, and still get out of it a functioning and fully alive human being. Asking a woman not to feel is harder than asking her not to breathe.

When I was trained at work on 'Trauma and young children: What every Early Childhood Educator needs to know,' the presenter showed me a completely different way of managing my emotions. How uninformed I had been regarding trauma and how my biases and my ignorance on the subject had actually made me insensitive to the people around me. Also, how my mind had only been working with what I knew, and I had not been aware of so many other things that I did not know. For example,

I didn't know a lot about trauma, so I took this webinar to learn and educate myself on the topic, thinking my learning on the topic would help me at work. Actually, her presentation completely changed my view and my understanding of my entire world. She was a role model for empathy and understanding and many times I have gone over and over the recording in order to understand how this is relevant to a bipolar mind like mine.

This is the problem that my TRIPOLAR mind has: my mind is like the Singing Sands of Tobermory, my favourite town in north Ontario. I have ten cms of depth in an ocean of knowledge. Yes, I am a master "organiza-tor" not an organizer because there is a difference. I am very messy with my stuff when my mind is at work and only have time to organize my stuff when my mind is at ease. I see the mess and it bothers me, but I give it the blind eye and wait because sometimes, writing is more important. I can't cook while I am writing because cooking takes time, which takes me away from my train of thought. I feel hungry, because my brain uses all my energy in the development of this train of thought. I eat to have more energy and because I am writing I don't exercise. Not exercising makes me slow and I gain weight because I only eat and sit, eat and sit, eat and sit. This is the way I get things done and not a recommended pattern. It is actually a vicious cycle that can drive people nuts because then the house looks messy and while I am aware of that, if I focus on cleaning, the inspiration will die.

My admiration goes to my family, who understanding where I was, were cooking and cleaning this last week for me. This is the fulfilment of the proverb: "You reap what you sow." When I was not in this writer's rush, I made sure they had a schedule for meals, and because I was on my night owl schedule, we switched around the times for meals. While culminating exams were online, I prepared food. Now it was time to switch and to give back. I am a lucky mom. Reciprocating is the premise for service and solidarity. We help one another, we are a team.

Inspiration comes to me in waves, like when you yawn and you feel tired, ready for a nap, but if you don't close your eyes to sleep, it passes by. You need to wait for the next cycle of tiredness and fatigue. This has been a crucial learning in my bipolar journey. Sleep counts and is absolutely necessary for my balance and well-being. It is one of those cases of what comes first the egg or the chicken? If I don't sleep, the bipolar hits. But wait, one time it wasn't like that. It was the opposite. I could not sleep because the bipolar was starting to hit. See the dilemma? It was not because I didn't sleep that my mind was active, it was because my mind was active that I could not sleep. This ends up being a riddle.

This is why my medications are my balance. I keep writing and writing, but when I start yawning, I go to my room, grab my medications and take them with a full glass of water. I do this because I know now that this is when my body starts crashing. Then I work for a few more hours or maybe less, but I fall asleep in the peaceful realm of my un-swinging or better, not-swinging reality. Had I not taken my medication at the first yawn, I would have missed the sleep cycle. Before I discovered that, I would have had a chocolate bar or some kind of sweet that gave me a sugar rush to stay awake, and that would have spun my mind around and added to the already excessive rhythm that the bipolar spike had. Sometimes, because I am cautious, I miss out on things such as wonderful words and phrases of inspiration. I have come to terms with that because no brilliant thought can bring me back into that constant and subtle rhythm that I have discovered to be the balance of my bipolar mind. My balance is to be able to oscillate between my lowest highs and my highest lows. The goal is to reach a point where I cannot notice the difference.

This has been such a discovery that is so effective that most people could not tell I am bipolar. This balance, a kind of quiet normality, acquired by temperance, loses its disguise when they see me taking notes or talking fast and linking ideas one with another. Relating to this can be difficult if you have not had the experience of a hyperactive-mind. Two myths we need to break regarding the mind are as follows: the fact that our minds are not able to multi-task and the fact that our minds sometimes need to be ignored in order to help them function at their best. I say this because we need to think about what we think. Yes, think of what our mind is thinking. Someone said once that "your mind is the crazy lady of the house." In my house, this is pretty much a settled truth.

As we apply rules to the way we treat others, we need to apply those same rules when we talk to ourselves. Yes, how am I treating myself and what am I saying to myself? Is it TRUE? Is it HELPFUL? Is it INSPIRING? Is it NECESSARY? Is it KIND? THINK. What kind of internal dialogue do I have? Am I saying to myself things that I would never even consider saying to my neighbours, or my friends or to someone else? TAME YOUR MIND. You are the master of your mind, the mastermind, master before the mind. People have learned to do that for generations. How can we do that? Put your mind to work on something so that it does not take over and drive you nuts. Television does not work for me. If I want to tame my mind, I need television plus music plus crochet. I need a TRIO to be able to get my mind locked-in and to put its unsettling influence to rest. How do I know when my mind is at ease? It is quiet. I feel the quiet and I can really hear myself think.

This is the amazing gift of the human mind. The capacity we all have to think, create and decide, all in one. Feelings lead our mind and put it to work. Am I hungry? I can cook (think), a delicious dinner (create) made of meat and veggies (decide). We make millions of decisions a day, some are physiological tasks that we don't even notice. For me waking up and getting out of bed, triggers a million nerve connections that go from my mind (think) to my extremities (create movement) and decide where to go. The myth of multitasking is not real. Humans cannot multitask. It is impossible for us to do two things at the same exact time. We can be great at SEQUENCING; we think and our minds create a sequence of actions and reactions. We don't perform thirty functions at once. We do one after the other in a matter of milliseconds. How long does it take for my mind to tell my fingers to write these words? It takes an absolutely minimal part of a billionth of a second, but I can only type one letter at a time on my keyboard to make a word. When I rush, mistakes happen. The muscle memory we have is miraculous. Just switch from the computer that you normally use to another one and try to type as fast as you are used to on your own keyboard. The mind needs time to adjust to that subtle, yet important alteration of the same experience.

My point is our minds can do only one thing at a time. You either talk or eat, you either move one way or another. We can't even sneeze with our eyes open. What we can be is excellent TASK SWITCHERS. This concept brought peace to my mind. It was on one of the GREAT COURSES DVDs that I got to help my kids go through high school and get great grades. We must have watched it a few times. This changed my paradigm and reassured me my mind was still subjected to my will and my desires. I was not just an automatic being doing all at the same time without control. Even in my more active days, my mind was following a sequence and an order. Knowing this, I learned to tame my mind. Because if stress made it wacko, the background music I put on and the use of my hands doing crochet slowed down its infinite desire to spiral out of control.

This is why the concept by Dr. Grecco is the secret to taming your bipolar mind. If you discover your bipolar gift, if you see that being bipolar is just the discovery and the acknowledgement that there is a gift you have to unravel, you start treating yourself kindly. Your mind, instead of becoming your worst enemy, becomes your ally in the unraveling of the gift. Here is the key. Ask yourself: Is it the arts? Is it singing? Is it writing? Is it birdwatching? It may even be when we sit to look at the world around us, quietly and in peace. If that is our bipolar gift, being able to sit and observe what happens around peacefully, will tame your mind.

Easily said, not that easily done. All this needs to sink in and be put into practice. Whether you read this because you are bipolar or not, it is a lot of information and a lot of concepts put together at once. None of this is written in stone. None of this is advice, a set method, or a treatment. It is the sharing of thoughts that each of us can then take in or discard. I am aware that all that we read, see, feel, smell and taste creates a response. I hope that these ideas grouped together shed some light into the mastermind we all possess. And by the way, I am far from keeping this rhythm of coherent–though abundant–train of thought. While writing these pages, I already broke the don't-eat-chocolate rule twice, had a full lentil-rice meal, and did not take my meds at the first yawn, because if I had done that, I would have stopped my train of thought in its tracks and lost the momentum, with the inertia hitting my TRIPOLAR mind. My music is on, and I am working side by side on two computers. I have proved my point to myself because all this time my hyper mind switched tasks gently, without making me feel unsettled. I just went with the flow, not too harsh on myself, constant, letting my highs be lows and my lows be as normal as I would like them to be.

This is my rollercoaster ride. I have to get enough energy to keep growing while learning to pace myself in a way that all the information I am holding inside, redirects itself. I am putting, unconsciously, all these different pieces of information into a funnel that, with some days of sleep and a few hours where I can relax my mind, create a flow. This concept has changed over the years. I am not the same person both physically and mentally. My younger years were quite simple and uneventful. A regular life in an extensive family, making our family gatherings over 100 people. This was the norm, to cook for many, to care for many. What was hard, was living alone, and only cooking for two or three. I've had a happy life, many tears shed, still very happy.

I do not believe that the secret to happiness is to never expect anything from anyone. That makes no sense to me. Maybe this makes sense to a plant or a tree. Being disappointed, sadly is a part of life. I once thought that my life was a tragedy, a tragic comedy that happened over and over again. With time, I have come to realize that it is a freakishly, amazing MUSICAL in which I get to choose what and when to dance. I set the tone and the rhythm that

I want to follow, and I decide how to follow the songs that are magically played for me to dance.

I did not include this in the acknowledgements, and I have to say it now as it shows where my heart is. Nothing I have written so far would be possible if it hadn't been for the unconditional, constant and abundant love of my Mom and my Dad. They mean the world to me, and I love them deeply.

8

An Invisible Diagnosis.

Another organization that keeps popping up on my Facebook, thanks to that "algorithm" or whatever obscure power they have to track our data, is called NICABM.COM. They talk about trauma, as well as fear, anger, shame, loneliness, depression and rejection. These are BIG, BIG emotions. They are the emotions that we'd like to hide, thinking that by ignoring them or putting them under the carpet they will leave us, and we will feel alright. They don't ever leave. These emotions slowly eat us up, destroy our confidence and make us question who we really are. These are invisible emotions because they attack us from the inside out. We have to stop trying to keep all these emotions inside because that inner struggle magnifies and has a debilitating effect on us. Yes, these emotions break our spirit and leave us vulnerable. So as NICAMB explains, when we see these emotions, we see the fears we have and there is something physiological behind it. These feelings physically affect us and can make an imprint on our nervous systems. That, I believe, is what we call trauma.

We have to learn to be gentle with ourselves. As we should not judge an institution by its faults, we should not judge ourselves by our mistakes. If we do, we leave no space for growth and improvement. We are rational and logical creatures who think. We cannot ignore our faults but what we can do is work at acknowledging them, thinking of ways to accept them and do reparation if it's possible, and if there is ground for it. Run deeply to the grounds of repentance. As Canadians, we are quite good at saying "sorry, sorry, sorry . . . I am soooo sorry." The more "o's" on the second sooooooorry, the worse you feel about it. It is the acknowledgement of our own faults and showing we regret whatever happened, not only a bit but a lot, what matters.

Our emotions have a direct effect on our body. These bodily reactions can go from sweat to tears, and from impulses we can't control to a complete shutdown of our defense system and our responses. Nature is the perfect example of this cause and effect. A rainstorm brings fear but at the same time, this water is needed for trees, plants and grass to grow. No rain equals no growth. I still remember that beautiful and gentle participant on

'American Idol' presenting her own song, singing like an angel. Although she was battling a sickness she said, "You cannot wait for life to stop being hard to be happy." Wow. A moment of despair is a lost moment, not because it was not happy, but because it kept us away from being happy. And happiness is something you create on your own when you are aware of who you are and how valuable you are.

We have to learn and re-learn how not to be overwhelmed by the feelings our body experiences with our change of emotions. We need to feel comfortable in our own skin and our skin, as it has different tones, holds different feelings. The spelling keeps underlining all my "We have to" and suggests changing it to "must." I see a huge difference between something you must do and something you have to do. The word must, seems to me optional: you must do or must not do . . . The "HAVE to" is for me a call to immediate, deliberate action. It represents a sense of urgency. That is the reflection I would like to bring out from this riddle of words and ideas tangled and untangled by this TRIPOLAR mind. You are the owner of your own reality. The complexity of our thoughts and feelings is sometimes overwhelming, but at some point, we really need to take charge of the headquarters of your mind and stand strong. Stay strong, step up our game to make a change.

If you are fluctuating between highs and lows, have broken relationships, keep wandering between the moods and the feelings of frustration and despair, loneliness and inadequacy, then you are being led either by fear, sadness, anger or unbelief. Those are valid emotions because we experience them whether we want it or not. However, never forget that there is another side to all we feel. Like there is day to night, you can feel cold or hot. Remember you can't have day and night at the same time or feel cold and hot at the same time. You can regulate these opposing feelings. You can be on a quest to reach peace and joy and get to a calm and gentle place where your spirit regains its strength and your weakness is turned into power. EMPOWER. Yes, we need to move onto empowering people so they can see where they are at, where they don't want to be and make the resolution to move toward the direction they desire. Resolve to be happy. We owe this to ourselves.

Learn your truth and re-learn how to live with your struggles. Sometimes we choose not to take the medications that can help us be better, but we end up drowning ourselves in coffee, chocolate, wine and in the worst cases drugs and promiscuity. Something that has been very clear to me all my life is that if I am in emotional pain, the last thing I need is wine, drugs or sex. These end up being the beginning of emotional decay, instead of comfort.

Re-learn your own patterns of behaviour. If at this point you think changing is easy, I can tell you, you need a heck of a lot of patience, resilience and most of all compassion for yourself, to be able to walk away from the patterns of behaviour that hurt you. If one glass of wine didn't help you, a bottle of wine won't either. You might feel numb, excited or great for a bit, but the low afterward will cost you three more bottles. If you put drugs in the picture, because they make you feel great or better, and unable to feel the pain, you are on a very dangerous slope. Wine plus drugs, and you are now entering the detox zone because now your body is poisoned twice. First by the pain of the emotions and now with the added challenge of overcoming an addiction.

Lean on people that you trust. Trust the people you love. Lean on one another but always be mindful that your mental health, and the state in which you are, is not their responsibility. It is very hard for them to understand what you are going through. They are scared too. I mean, let's be sincere, being on a high mood and I mean a natural high, no drugs or stimulants present—feels awesome. Not everyone can handle it and becomes an obstacle, a threat. It is the lack of understanding between people that care for each other that ruins the relationships. Why? This is because instead of trying to understand how the other person is feeling, we react. We just assume they are judging us or that they don't care enough to try to understand us. We are not communicating well. We end up feeling misunderstood and not being validated.

Following your doctor's advice is the first direction to keeping you well. Keep your promises to self-care and help yourself. When you get there, you will find your own rhythm and get to your peaceful place, then you will understand more and more how self-destructive the swinging is. It depletes our energy and ruins our relationships. Your rhythm is the most needed and required seatbelt on the rollercoaster of your life.

I don't live alone, but I am alone, by myself on this journey. I live surrounded by amazing and loving people, but I am on my own. Please don't fear that. It is my journey and I get to decide my itinerary, the times of travel and the times of rest. At the end, our journey is only ours and we are the ones traveling from the first moment to the last. Accepting who I am, how much I have changed and forgiving myself for my faults, my mistakes and my shortcomings, has let me move forward. I have become a stronger person learning that others were on their own journey too. Maybe there is nothing to forgive about the way life unraveled, because otherwise, I wouldn't be the woman I am today. I consider myself a regular woman. I am an advocate for the feminine genius expressed in such a beautiful way by St. John Paul the Great in his explanation of 'Theology of the Body.' He is my hero. His photograph is on a bookshelf in my room and it reminds me of the unending love for humanity that was in his heart. If I could choose someone to spend a day with, it would be him. In this ideal encounter, I would love to go on a ski trip with him in the Alps, as that was one of his favourite sports. I believe I might be too old now to really enjoy fully the experience of skiing, but I keep trying. I've tried the last three years, but age is age, and flexibility and leg strength has changed with time, especially because I don't workout consistently. I've come to terms with that reality, and the fact that I can have lots of fun even if I stay in the smaller hills, that for me, feel like black diamonds.

John Paul II's 'Theology of the Body' helped me to understand the responsibility that I have to see myself and my physical body as a gift. It helped me understand how I can, in many ways, be a gift to others. When we fail and miss the mark, this is where we grow and learn the most. Only if I learn from my mistakes and have the resolution to not keep doing the same things over and over, will I mature and grow. I need to move from feeling repentance and real sorrow for my shortcomings, into forgiveness. I realize that real healing comes from living in the present moment, as we are incapable of going back in time and changing things we did, to others and to ourselves.

9
Believe in Yourself.

"Nadie es monedita de oro para que todo el mundo lo quiera". A blunt truth; not everyone is a golden coin for everyone to like it. This is a literal translation that at some point I will be able to adapt to the English language so its meaning is better understood. Really, you are not the golden ticket that everyone wants to have, so believe in who you are. You are precious.

Easy to say, but not so easily done. Why do you have to do it? Because others believe in you. If you want to skip over this chapter, you won't miss anything. It has live examples of my journey. Writing this book has not been a linear experience. It has actually been kind of messy. It includes tangled and scattered pieces put together with a purpose, like a puzzle, but you are not the one building it, you are the one designing it. My life, until 2017, was the regular life of an insignificant inhabitant of this world. What I mean is that I am just one more person among billions of people: one tiny shell in the ocean, a drop of water in Niagara Falls. It is sometimes unclear how simple it is to see our place in the world. We live, we die. But it is in this living that we find our purpose. So, to contrast with this littleness, this is what I believe we are. We are hikers going on a journey through the mountains of our lives. Do we sit down and think: "I am one in a billion, I am stopping here?" NO. Why? Because in the story of my life, I am all the time on scene. I am the main character, the protagonist. I am the one that stays beginning to end, no matter what the plot of the story is.

As I am writing and putting together my ideas, I check my phone: first my messages, then Facebook, Instagram, and then back to Facebook and Instagram again. As if in five minutes those social platforms would change the content I see. I mean, those platforms are, in full honesty, successful because of the people on them. They are amazing tools and in the last two years have served us well. There have been a lot of discussions lately because of, or thanks to, that "algorithm" or whatever obscure power they have to track our data. The more you go in and like people, the more you are exposed and see things related to what you liked previously. I actually noticed beside the advertisements a feature that says: "because you interacted with a post from. . . ." I went back and asked to remove the messages because

I wasn't really interested in the "extras." I was interested in the post that I was directly choosing and interacting with, nothing else. Those additions mortify and actually derail me. Why? Because the algorithm is conditioned and assuming what I want and who I am. When I buy shoes, I don't want to see more shoes. I don't need to see more of what I bought. It uses patterns, not psychology. I had already made a purchase and it screws up my mind because now I see all the products on sale. I see all the other options I did not search for or saw before. I bought what I bought. Period. It is frustrating. How do I recover and get myself back together? I go, manually, one by one, post by post and discard them. NOT INTERESTED. I do it over and over hoping one day the algorithm will finally understand my reasoning and leave my memories alone.

What I often do is take screenshots of motivational quotes in friends' posts. I also love nature. The sky has a special meaning for me, so I take pictures of it regularily. I love the changes in the seasons, and I also document that with pictures. I document my life experiences on my Facebook. I post family celebrations, special moments and vacations with a private profile. I am grateful today that I have actively been posting things. The computer with all the pictures of my family and kids growing up was an old portable Mac. The videos of our family road trips around the US and Canada and the videos when my puppies were born all got lost when I gave the computer to my son. When he asked me if he could erase everything,

I said yes. I was naïve. I thought only the documents that I had saved on a USB were going to disappear, rather than all my photos and videos of a lifetime. Oh well, my mistake, I have got to learn to let go and suck it up. I have to stick only to the memories in my mind.

Some things worry me, especially after seeing a few movies like 'The Notebook' and another movie in which a wife goes into a retirement residence because of an onset of Alzheimer's. She forgets who her husband is and starts spending time with another man. What a sad scene when the husband goes into her room with flowers, and she doesn't know who he is, so she starts screaming for help. A broken heart, perfectly played by the actor, made that situation come to life. My admiration to the actress too, because realizing that you have to act like a person that is this sick must be hard. Maybe, as the first movie showed, we all should write the story of our lives, not as a biography, but as a chronical to which we can refer as we age. Please tell me, how many of you wish you had asked your grandparents or parents more about their lives? Everything stays in the heart, but in the mind? The memory fails. Those treasures stay hidden and can get lost in the realms of our minds.

Someone told me: "You have to write this book in Spanish." I thought about it, but I can't. My TRIPOLAR mind exists only in English because of what I mentioned before, my desire to adapt and to take in every second of my experiences in Canada. That is also why you find a few words in Spanish without being translated. I apologize but the feeling that word expresses to me in Spanish does not exist in English. Here are quite a few examples of that. The first example is the word chipmunk. We know that a chipmunk and a squirrel are not the same species. Chip & Dale and Alvin in Spanish are considered the same species, we call both Ardillas. In Spanish, my feet have fingers–dedos de los pies–in English, they are toes. Can you imagine how many times I confused people by saying feet fingers? This one is a gem. When we eat something and it upsets our stomach really badly, and we are not able to go to work, we call it food poisoning in English. In Spanish we are intoxicated–una "intoxicación". Intoxicated in English is "borracho" in Spanish–how they call you when you've had way too many drinks. So, when my colleague called my boss to tell her she was not coming to work because she was intoxicated, you should have seen her face. I was so glad I already knew what was happening and I was in the office with her when she received the text. The look on her face was of disbelief. How can you call your boss, say you are sick and say that so . . . "descaradamente"? (Well, that word does not exist in English–the closest is shamelessly but actually it means your face fell down of shame.) I explained the difference, she was not drunk but ill of her stomach, and she laughed. I can go on and on, with Latin expressions that do not exist in the English language.

Also, my thoughts are quite colourful and too much sometimes. Some people say, "You are so extra." If I took all this "EXTRA" from the book, it would not have the powerful meaning it has for me. You might read or put this book down because it is too much or too boring, uninteresting, unrelatable to you, and I can go on and on. Those are my insecurities. I don't expect it to be perfect for everyone because that is impossible, I am doing my best to share my knowledge. "Lo perfecto es enemigo de lo bueno" in an English translation: "The perfect is an enemy of the good." If you have come this far, I hope you are not disappointed. I fear rejection and I fear the criticism that these thoughts will bring. Because I am so aware my experiences are limited by my own understanding of what happened to me. Yes, you read it well: me, me, me. This book is the result of "Me being with myself and I." If I sell many copies, it will be great. If I touch one soul in pain because of the bipolar diagnosis, it will mean the world to me. If a family understands a little bit better what this diagnosis entails, I can die in peace, because great pain came because of my incapacity to understand where I was and who I was, with this gift inside of me.

I think, and it won't be a lie, if my life had stayed the same, I would not be telling this story. I have tried to be clear while writing my story. At one point I had to realize that I had to write what needs to be written. I am apologetic in advance, because what I have learned is that there is not only one truth. There is my truth, your truth and the REAL, OBJECTIVE truth is somewhere in the middle. My biggest flaws have been not in what I say but in the way I deliver that message. And by delivery I am not talking about how it gets to you (via email, Facebook, text). The delivery is in the tone and in the way it makes you feel when you read it or when you listen to me.

Your mind can be your worst enemy. Between what we hear, what we really understand and take in, there are three different realities. All I can say is that in my day-to-day, I try to live my reality fully aware of how it affects others. This changed my understanding of my life so please, be an advocate for yourself. I found four recordings done in October 2018, December 2018, and January 4 and 6 of 2019. I discovered these recordings when I started voice recording, to write this book. There were four voice memos from the past that showed my mindset, fear, anger, and desperation. These were difficult to listen to, but I needed to listen and reflect on how I was feeling at that time.

They shocked me. When I found them on a summer evening, I pressed play. I started listening and I had to stop. I had to go and do something else. I knew that those words and especially the tone of my voice varied immensely and was so different from my mindset today. The first one I listened to was recorded on December 4, 2018 and there I acknowledged, "I am at the onset of depression" I tell you; it was hard to hear myself worried and something brought back the feelings inside. That is why I had to stop. I could not listen to the recording in the middle of the night. It would have affected me if I left those thoughts inside my mind overnight. I could hear it in the morning, and I actually went over it several times. It was so enlightening but put me on a setback. It caused a hiatus from writing that lasted two weeks. I was emotionally and mentally affected by what I heard. It was me, but with a totally different mindset. It was my reality at that time. It sounded real. All of this moved my writing plans and derailed my schedule, putting all my deadlines off track.

Listening to those recordings, I could see how wounded I was emotionally and how hard it was to deal with those feelings of fear, unworthiness, and uncertainty, when I was down. On the other hand, it reassured me that my journey had been successful. I could now see myself with kinder eyes. I still feel vulnerable sharing my vulnerability out loud. But as I said, I had to do it if I wanted to write this book.

10

You've Got It!

IT IS ALL INSIDE OF YOU. Only you can work on yourself. Breathe and do nothing. Yes, just breathe and do nothing else. Activism and unsettledness are the perfect environment for your mind to go wild. When you learn to settle your mind and distinguish between your inner voice and your inner struggle, you will find peace. Since I learned that I can keep my mouth shut and my ears open—because we have only one mouth and two ears—I found something I did not know. Less is more and that nothing is not the absence of things, but everything.

This is not a call to be lazy and turn into a couch potato. This is a call for action in the hardest thing that a human being can do, and that is to quiet the mind. We react to stimuli. We have an animal instinct and are led by our emotions. All is good. What is hard, is to determine what we are going to do with how we feel. Stephen R. Covey in his book "Daily reflections for Highly effective People. Living 'The 7 habits of highly effective people,' every day" said it well. The reflection for April 14 says: "Between stimulus and response, one has the freedom to choose." I summarize it like this: between the action and the reaction, there is a space. In that space lays your happiness.

Yesterday my friend Alexandra Montealegre, my Colombian twin from different parents, was telling me about this. And wow, it clicked and guided me to write this chapter. Go for a walk but do nothing. Look around but do nothing. Sit to eat and do nothing. It is hard at the beginning because we are used to running in constant action in our frenetic lives—some more than others. We are afraid of silence. These last days, I write and do nothing. I am moving my fingers and my eyes, following the keyboard and checking the screen. I have the music on, listening to Fleetwood Mac, my son is walking around getting ready to go out, but I am doing nothing. I am just present, aware of the sounds outside: the people driving in their cars, the construction workers in the corner. All that I can hear, see and feel. Still, I am doing nothing. There is noise, things are out of place, but I am reflecting. I am in a state of contemplation and from this "nothing," comes great peace and deep thoughts.

When I feel overwhelmed, I try to take really BIG deep breaths. Pacing your breathing is crucial at childbirth, when swimming and when you are underwater. It is a function that we do without even noticing, but when we notice, it has a deeper meaning. You breathe or you die. In my case, I hyperventilate a lot. Behind my mask, I can see the ins and outs of my own breath. If I am hyperventilating, getting nervous and rushing doesn't help at all. To prove my point, I just had to stop my peaceful nothing to get ready to go out and pick up some glasses at the optometrist, renew a health card and get pictures for a passport. Only thinking of those things got my mind going. So much to do, so little time. The actions contrasted with the peaceful hours in which I had been writing these lines. I am intense. I am tense. I am stressed, and I haven't even stopped writing. This is a very characteristic trait of my bipolar mind. I get freaked out very easily. I am like a match you light that heats up fiercely. It's not that a fierce flame is bad, it is the intensity by which it is done and the way it affects people's lives. As a fire can keep us warm, it can be used to protect us from danger. It is a form of energy. It can also destroy with its power.

What you do with the power you have is what really matters. You can use a flame to be a light, or you can use it to burn something down to ashes. Your personal decisions are what lead to an outcome that is either good or bad. I know good and bad are two opposing terms but sometimes, if I don't use extreme concepts as an example, I can't really prove my point. The power of the mind is what has brought this world into the technological and medical development of today. It is more than obvious during this COVID-19 pandemic that we are resilient, that we have suffered a lot, and we will continue to suffer with the unknown. However, these sufferings have brought out the determination, the solidarity and the immense capability of adapting to unknown circumstances. When we look back at the dark and difficult days we have been living in the past two years, I hope we do so with reflection, not with judgement.

While waiting for your peaceful self to emerge, be patient with yourself. Time heals everything and teaches everything. Time is the master. I have received the greatest practical advice: "If you step on shit, you don't go back to step on it again." In very crude Spanish: "Cuando uno pisa mierda, uno no se devuelve a pisarla." This means to stop dwelling on your past mistakes. They suck. Don't dwell on what you cannot change and move on. Keep on walking. There is always something to learn and things will get better if we want them to get better. We have willpower and decision power. Make a choice.

11

Time tells All.

When your mind finally lands on a secure and balanced place—for me a place guaranteed by my rigorous use of medication—you will be able to see the good and the bad without fear. You will be able to reflect and take in your experiences, then put them together so you can help others. You will stop fearing to live, and most importantly, you will be able to stop using drugs, chocolate and wine as excuses to feel better. You need to feel better because of you, your journey and your acceptance of who you are and what you've been through.

This summer of 2021 is my summer of reflection. The summer of 2020 was my summer of self-discovery. Now I know that the summer of 2022, God willing, is when I will finally embark on the boat that will take me through the waters of my unique and personal journey. Where is it taking me? Well, to reach the purpose of my life. I hope the year will be the culmination point where I will finally be able to reach out and reach further to make my dreams become a reality.

"Success is never linear. It looks more like scribbles." I read this at work. This is a very mindful quote put up for us as inspiration and to help us not get discouraged when things go wrong. I know my life is a page full of unended phrases and unfinished projects. There are many good intentions with no results and many moments that I wish I had lived with the insights of today. Having 20-20 vision could have made these projects very cool and an amazing reality. Well, this amazing reality might have existed only in my mind because we are surrounded by lots of people. People like me, that feel, think and decide. This is where reality kicks in because when we lose the connection with our fellow beings and are focused only on ourselves, we miss so much and we don't even notice it. Only when I've had my bipolar "attacks," have I been able to connect more deeply with my inner being. It's like having an out-of-body experience. You see the world you live in with awe and a different perspective, similar to orbiting around the world in a space shuttle.

I already spoke about my first bipolar episode, in summer of 2005. In the summer of 2012, I had my second one and surprisingly I could see exactly the same pattern as with the first one. It was exactly the same pattern. I was in awe and could not stop "dreaming," yes dreaming because I could relive the same attack but with my full consciousness. What a gift! This attack was triggered by a very different cause: having too much fun. Yes, that is why we are so addicted to our highs, because they are awesome. Please note, I will never refer to a bipolar high as the state you reach when you use recreational drugs, I have never and will never do drugs. My home country suffered so much from the war on drugs and there is so much violence and inequality due to that horrendous problem. This is the thing. When people did not know me, when I said I was from Colombia, they immediately made a remark about drugs. As always, my big mouth led the way. "Colombians? We don't do drugs. We are not drug addicts. It is you guys who use the drugs and waste your lives using them." I felt offended, deeply offended by this bias. And it is true. You might find some Colombians who fall in that unreal world of addictions but that is not the norm. We are way beyond that.

The fun that ignited this new bipolar high was actually caused by rollercoasters: not of emotions, but real rollercoasters. The kids were teens, we got the Season Pass to Canada's Wonderland and that was the highlight of our summer. We could go at any time plus the kids could go even with friends up to the Halloween Hunt. We had visitors and what a better way to get through the summer than visiting an amazing amusement park. So, we went weekly. We got there early and ran to the Leviathan and the Behemoth first. Before getting on the rides, I took a small dose of motion sickness syrup for children. In this way, I could go at the pace of my teenage children. We went three or four times in a row, up-and-down those crazy rides. I could feel the adrenaline in my veins, my stomach going up and down in the same way that my arms were going up and down. The excitement took over and turned into a new bipolar high. I was so full of adrenaline and full of dopamine that it spiked this high. I realized it and as a positive soul, I was ecstatic: nervous, but ecstatic. I had a chance to relive all those feelings and understand them. It was a discovery to me. I isolated myself and warned everyone around me. "Mom is having a bipolar attack," I said proudly. I could document it and follow it with my conscious mind.

I moved out of my room that had too many stimuli: the TV, the doors, the bathroom lights, the fan above the bed. It was too big. I had too much space and I was not sure I could manage. I was like a new puppy when you get it home. I had to be contained in a safe space: something small and manageable. I needed to be in a place I trusted, away from everyone. I still remember walking around the block and telling my husband, "I am having a bipolar attack, if you see me doing something weird, or not looking at you face to face, with my eyes on your eyes, call 911." I wasn't sure how it was going to unravel. It was scary. I just wanted to give it a try and see how this new episode in a controlled situation would unravel.

My safe place was my son's room. It had a single bed against the wall with a desk and a small window with some blinds. I could make the room dark with no other stimuli or distractors. I grabbed the phone. Yes, I had a landline, that was part of who I was. This number was the home phone that anyone could call to get hold of us before iPhones existed. I also grabbed a notebook, a pen, and some water. I called my doctor and asked for advice and asked for the way in which my meds would help me. The answer was simple, take your bedtime meds now, sleep well and call me in the morning. That was easy and I was willing to embrace what was to come.

I called my mom, my sisters and my best friends from Canada and Venezuela, I needed to let them know what was going on. They always cared for me and this was the time I needed their support. Our kids were friends and if anything happened, I needed their help and the peace of mind of sending my children somewhere, where I knew they would feel safe. It was a nerve-wracking experience for all of us. I let the five bipolar days pass. In between, I was writing endless notes in that notebook. Do I still have it? Yes. Am I ready to go over those notes now? No. That has to wait because that will be another adventure. Another book, another "surprise" to discover.

My bipolar episode of that summer ended a week later. I was flying back to Colombia for a family wedding. I felt in control when I left Canada on a plane. The moment

I stepped off that plane onto the soil of my homeland, the high disappeared making space for wonderful family time where mental illness didn't stand a chance. In Colombia, my safe and beautiful haven, I am never bipolar.

12

Be proud of being Bipolar.

We have been so wrongly labeled as bipolar. Labeled is different from being diagnosed. I can be diagnosed with cancer, but I am not the cancer. I can be diagnosed with diabetes, but I am not the diabetes. In all sicknesses, and I do not consider myself an expert, there is a diagnosis followed by a treatment and a follow up.

In my case, my diagnosis was followed by lots of appointments until I was medicated with the right medicine and the right dose. This is what sometimes we do not realize. Those medications can change over time because as human beings we change, we age and we keep evolving. This is a hard reality. We are not static. We need permanent counselling, psychiatric assessments and, more than anything, we need to trust the people that are here to help us. We mistrust so much the doctors and the people that are professionally capable of helping us. We are actually difficult patients. For some time, I went to my psychiatrist appointments with a whole list of feelings and concerns and when I was sitting in front of my psychiatrist, I was another person. I was okay. I "managed" the appointments really well and suddenly, the moment I got out, when I was alone, by myself, I realized the I-am-okay attitude that I had in the medical office was far from the reality. I was again anxious or in despair. I had been with my doctor for five minutes or five hours and it did not show how I really was feeling. This frustration became a more and more unbearable situation as I realized it was in the intimacy of my home, that the bipolar traits magnified, creating tension.

I would arrive home after the appointment feeling already defeated and hopeless, pretending to be better or okay at least, but inside I knew something was not right. It was then that writing became a therapy, an outlet for my pain and a way to remove the emotional pain and the confusion I was feeling in my body. Don't get me wrong, it wasn't writing like I am doing now, with full consciousness of where I want to go and where I am at. I would actually call it journaling, as it really focused on writing the emotions of the moment. Why? Because by the time I saw my psychiatrist again, I would think I was okay, and I was not.

My journal is my reality check. It is more valuable than all the money I have in my bank account. It was really what helped me grow in the consciousness of where I was emotionally and how that was affecting my behaviours and my life. Why? Because I could journal exactly what I was feeling at that moment. I noted the date and time I was writing and also, the background; what was worrying or affecting me at that time and how I felt about it. I could go back and read it when I was okay or when I saw the doctor and it would be true and real. It has worked wonders in my life because I have learned to label, express and name my emotions as they come. I realized my bipolar condition is not cyclical, well, it was before menopause. It was integrally related to my fertility cycles and my periods. It was when menopause hit that my hormones turned wacko.

WE ARE WHO WE ARE. We can mature, make some needed changes, learn to be loving, accepting and willing to give the best, but our essence, who we are, how God made us, this does not change. You don't turn water into wine or oil. Water is the essence and will not change. You can dilute things, mix things but change the essence? Probably not. Maybe if I had frozen myself, as you freeze water into ice cubes it would have made a difference, but I doubt it. Ice turns into water again, and so does vapour. Look at the clouds; they can be white or grey. They turn from soft cotton balls into furious grey masses, viciously pouring water onto the earth. All this is to say, be proud of who you are. We are not golden coins that everyone would love to handle. This term "Nadie es monedita de oro para que todo el mundo lo quiera" means no matter how valuable you are, not everyone is going to like you, to give you the value that you have. Only you can know your worth.

What made my journey difficult was my determination to remain who I was despite having been diagnosed as a Bipolar II patient. For a short time, my diagnosis made me feel shameful. As I look back, I realize this fight to preserve my own identity despite being labeled Bipolar has brought me to where I am today.

I participated actively in a "Grief course" during my Pastoral Ministry Certification. That helped me to understand the turmoil I had inside of me. I had many losses in my life: people, relationships, jobs and immigration. Leaving my birth country became a loss I had to grieve, despite the wonderful opportunity and valuable life I've had living in Canada, the place I love and call my home. I just was not aware of that until now. When you have a loss, no matter how or where, it tears your soul apart. There are no words to alleviate the pain, yet at the beginning, the body and the brain become numb so you can cope with the situation. Then the pain awakens. You cry and faint. You wake up every day destroyed while healing and grieving takes its course. In our own life, we are all cooking our own grief soup. You must be wondering what that means.

Yes, a grief soup. This beautiful, animated video shown at my parish by the Grief Counselors, pictures an older woman who is placing the ingredients into her pot. The pantry was full of moments of grief, the ingredients for the soup. Whether you grieve the loss of a loved one, a friend, a job, a relationship, a pet, an opportunity missed, moving towns, losing something of great value, and we can go on, we all grieve many times in our life. Maybe it was a rejection at school or a test that went wrong, a diagnosis or an unexpected accident that had terrible consequences, all these cause us to grieve. I am not trying to generalize grief, just being aware of the many times we grieve, and it is not only for a person who has passed. We also grieve for the past, the present and the future. What it was, what it could have been and what it will never be. That is probably the hardest thing to accept, what we will not be able to become because of that loss. If you lose a child, the pain is unbearable, and grief takes over every area of your being. When you lose a parent, you know that in theory they leave before you. Still, the idea of not having them close to us, in our daily life makes this loss a very profound one, that requires years of grief and healing. If it is a relationship, we have to reroute our course, but the memories will never ever disappear.

The six-session course took us from the acceptance of the many losses in our lives, to honouring the memories we had inside. This was so moving and touching. When asked to share in small groups our loss. I started bawling. I could not breathe. I never realized how deep in my heart and my soul those loses were rooted. We tend to block those realizations because they make us weak and vulnerable. We tend to cover the void with superficiality, anger or hate. We try, by all means, to avoid the pain of knowing we have a loss and our heart is broken. This was a very well planned six-week course where all the stages of grief were looked at, shared and where many of us found peace and understanding.

I can still remember the lessons of each of the sessions of that grief course and thanks to my habit of taking notes on everything, I can go back and look into the notebook that I used for that specific group and read and remember what I learned and how I felt at that moment. Grief is a process, not a feeling. To grieve can take us as long as we need for our soul to heal. I felt so hopeful when the grief counsellor said that, "We grieve until we learn we can stand again on our own."

Wow, my grief was not a death sentence for my heart. It would heal, never forget, but I would be able to move on. When? Only time could tell. I definitely felt that was the most rewarding lesson from all this Pastoral Ministry experience. I could understand better the content and the depth of grief because I had been attending, learning and engaging like all those there. I realized that I was living with a broken heart. But I also understood that the healing process was happening. I was going through that process already, the process of accepting my losses and seeing new opportunities in my life. Grieving became more and more understandable to me when she mentioned that we not only grieve the loss of the person but that we grieve the loss of the relationship, and of the dreams and the aspirations we had with that person. It became crystal clear to me that I was starting to understand better how emotionally attached I was to many of the losses I had in my life. When I realized the impact, those losses had on my emotions and my mental health, I felt better and more human. I did not have to be strong and pretend to be well all the time. I could give myself time and permission to mourn.

It takes our own time to heal. I am not saying I don't feel anything anymore. Sometimes I get angry, disappointed or puzzled. Only writing this brings memories and I start feeling a bit unsettled. See how easy it is to get side-tracked by emotions? Writing is like time travel. You can go back in time and see, feel and remember what you went through. And it is okay. It is a good thing when you accept yourself as you are with all your feelings. You will still be okay if you get sad or happy or angry at something because guess what? Giving yourself permission to be imperfect and feel is one of the most important things to do in order to achieve mental freedom. Yes, mental health is the capacity you have to accept yourself for who you are, inside and out. Feeling is not what is wrong, it is what we do with those feelings. For me, I just spit them out and then dance. Yes, just writing this made me sick to my stomach, and that is okay. I am not afraid to feel in this uncomfortable way anymore. Why? Because I know a bit of music plus a few distractors will put me back where I was before these emotions started.

On my fiftieth birthday, I received not only the love of so many people which filled my heart and my soul, but I also got an upgrade in technology that I didn't expect and that now is the most amazing part of my life. My television was a Sony Bravia from the 2000s. It had a good resolution and image, I thought, but it was old. It was so old that my new internet provider could not make it work as the system was really outdated. It didn't accept any of the new AppleTV devices. My gifts were a new TV, a firestick and an Alexa that has upgraded and revolutionized my entertainment enjoyment. I had a very hard time at first because at my work they call me ALEXA. When I was talking on the phone and someone said, "Alexa, do this . . ." I felt yelled at, called into action. Well, now I boss around my Alexa. "Alexa, play Carlos Vives," "Alexa, play Enanitos Verdes," "Alexa, play boleros." Sometimes it doesn't get it but I have enjoyed the fact that when I am alone, sometimes I yell and someone answers without any complaints.

Learn to live in peace with the invisible. Your visible self is an image of your invisible truth. When I am not okay, you can see it. I slack. You will see me with no makeup and my hair a mess. I am dressed poorly, and it is all right. It is probably the greatest lesson from this COVID-19 pandemic. We are so vulnerable. We need social interaction and to be able to get out and live. Being locked inside, by ourselves, is not a way of living.

13

How do we change the Stigma?

We need to change the way we talk about mental illness. This is again easily said, but so difficult to make a reality. What do I mean by change the stigma? Well, my idea is that we change our VOICE when we advocate for help and when we talk to people about our struggles. It was during the winter of 2017 that I had a clinically depressive episode. The moment I noticed something wasn't right, I went to my family doctor who medicated me with an anti-depressant in addition to the antipsychotic medication I had been taking for twelve years. It didn't go as well as I wanted because though it stopped the toxic train of thought I was experiencing, it was not compatible with my other prescribed medications. I started having palpitations and felt my heart was pounding. When she rectified the prescription and

I went to the pharmacist her words pounded in my head even louder than my heart. I explained how the first med prescribed was not working for me, and she refused to fill my new prescription saying: "If that medicine didn't hurt you, this one will." I don't know if those were her exact words or whether it is my extremely sensitive mind that is putting those words together, but that is what I understood. I was desperate and said, "Then what do I do?" I decided to stay with the first prescription, taking it every other day until I could see a psychiatrist.

This is where I want you to sit and reflect on your own mental health. We all have mental health issues because the mind, like any other organ is a part of our body. I don't know a man or woman who has not been extremely sad, extremely happy, serious, worried, concerned, motivated or empowered. All these emotions are part of a list of daily states of mind. We all have a kind of bipolarity, that is the fluctuation of our feelings and moods, not in public, but when we are on our own. Deep inside we can feel lonely, nothing can replace that feeling, that void. My decision when I was feeling down was to avoid talking about it. I did not give myself permission to dwell on it. I just put on a big smile and kept living. I learned to live with the ups and downs of my life. I learned that if I let myself be too low or too high, I would suffer. I would suffer much more because the oscillation between the good and the hard times is what makes my moods fluctuate.

I read an online article from uhhospitals.org titled "The Top 5 Most Stressful Life Events and How to Handle Them."

These are what they consider the five greatest stressors in life: death of a loved one, divorce, moving, major illness or injury and job loss. We all battle one or more of these in our life span, sometimes several of them at the same time. If you realize it, we are consistently battling stressors in our own reality. Physically we can be struggling with our health and mentally trying to adapt to our own circumstances. Whatever stress you go through puts you down and affects every single part of your being. You cannot pass a second of the day without feeling hurt or lonely. No matter how many people you have around. I had something very, VERY clear and if I was stressed, depressed, on my ups or downs, I would not rely on alcohol, sex or drugs to go through this. I was unwilling to even use coffee as a coping mechanism, because as hard as it is going through struggles "cold turkey," the oscillation between a sugar rush and a really down day would derail my well-being to the core.

This principle was handed to me by a great therapist I had when I was in the early stages of the diagnosis. The smaller the oscillation, the easier it is for my body to adjust to changes and respond to struggles. Picture a gas stove. You need to be really aware of how to ignite the pilot and how high the flame will be. That is why all stoves have control panels, so you can adjust them to different intensities. Apply this to your life. We need to be able to decide if we are going to live our lives on HIGH, MEDIUM or LOW. With this example I learned the difference between anger and anxiety. Anxiety is like a pot cooking pasta. You get the water to boil and throw the pasta in. I have the bad habit of adjusting the dial to high, so it boils faster. Stay with me on this last sentence. "I have the bad habit of adjusting the dial to high, so it boils faster." What temperature do you set the stove knob on? HIGH, MEDIUM or LOW? If I keep the dial on high while the pasta cooks, a white bubbly foam starts to grow, and grow, and grow. If I don't stop it on time, it overflows, spilling around the pot. That is anxiety. Our anxiety is caused by having the dial too high and when it spills? It spills onto your inner circle. The people around you, the close ones. You burn them out.

Let's talk about anger. This is one of the most extreme feelings, at least for me. Why? Because when I get angry, I open my mouth and literally burst all around. Anger is like a pressure cooker on that same high setting. The pressure starts building inside and if I don't stop it, it explodes. That explosion bursts all over our kitchen, making a huge mess. The term 'all over' refers to the people around you. That is what road rage is: putting yourself on HIGH and just exploding, messing everyone around. The driver that cut you off might not even know who you are or what happened to you, but you will enrage him or her so much that your HIGH burns out to the other and now two pressure cookers are driving irresponsibly. So, this pressure cooker explosion causes a disaster that requires twice the work and time to clean up the mess left. Sometimes we can't even clean up the mess because the consequences are irreversible. What is the solution to these anxieties and these angry moments? The answer is simple: learn to turn down the heat. Learn how and when to turn the dial of your responses down and decide to live in a setting you can control.

It is hard to know where you are at, but with some cognitive therapy and a lot of patience and kindness to yourself, you can start learning. Don't let people push your buttons. They don't have the right to do that. If they are the ones controlling the temperature of your life, you need to act. Do something because those buttons need to be controlled by you, the mastermind. This is only possible if you WANT to do it. I can reflect and reflect on my own reality but if I don't realize that it is the alcohol or the drugs that make me feel "okay," and that this is a fake okay, I will repeat the same pattern. No amount of help, support, or medication can put you out of it if you don't want to get out of it. I am an advocate for you and your mental health, but I also see the harm, the really selfish patterns we live by, because we become handicapped by our own illness. We shield ourselves, cover our unwillingness to change and be okay just by saying, "It is my mental illness."

I feel so bad having to bring that up. I was reading this book for the last time before sending it to the editor and I realized I had missed a part: a part that I wasn't even aware of. It came out on the last paragraph and is something I will be reflecting on as I write these lines. This is the interim of my two-act show. "We become handicapped by our own illness." We use it as a shield to protect us from anything that can harm us. A shield can be the walls of our house. A shield could be our clothing. A shield can be our car. All these have become armours that serve us and protect us from harm. An armour is a "protective layer over a body, vehicle, or other object intended to deflect or diffuse damaging forces." Is it possible that we put an armour on to protect us from the pain of being okay? or for not being able to accept our mistakes and shortcomings as ours but to justify them as a result of our illness? This is where calling it a condition, not a sickness, or a diagnosis makes a huge difference in the way we look at ourselves.

We can differentiate ourselves from the illness. I am not the flu, I have the flu. I am suffering from cancer, I am not a cancer. I am not the bipolar, I have been diagnosed with bipolar disorder, but I am actually TRIPOLAR. Here is where we have to remember, deeply, we are more than our struggles. We are more than our shortcomings. We are who we are despite our struggles and shortcomings. We will stop hiding behind this armour set up to "protect us" that becomes a hiding place. Can you imagine freeing yourself of the weight of that armour? Can you imagine being able to move freely away from the restrictions of your thoughts and the way people see you? Can you imagine being free of the shame and the guilt of having been diagnosed? It may seem unreal. It might not be possible yet, because we have to change the stigma. That stigma puts us behind a curtain of shame that deflects and diffuses who we really are. It magnifies the feelings of inadequacy because we think we are justified. Please, keep on reading, and give yourself the opportunity to have this information sink in. Rome was not built in a day. Many cities needed walls to protect them from danger.

Don't just bring your guard down. Start tearing down those walls, removing those barriers, that carcass that restricts you from being yourself. Turn this shell, the base of your being, into a framework that sustains your being, becomes your foundation and builds a solid structure that you can own. This will help you be yourself, and present it to the entire world. **Everyone around you deserves to see you for who you are.** You don't have to change. You just have to unfold and become familiar with your own being. When you are out of the armour, you will survive like a snail does. You will always be able to carry your shell with you. It is much lighter than the armour. You will learn to be comfortable out of the lows and highs, navigating life in the in-betweens. I like myself better when my highs and lows are not too high and not too low. Balance your act. Find that perfect balance. The rollercoaster ride can be enjoyed without having to be on those two extremes. You will be like a kid on the swings, laughing peacefully. You will be able to go on the seesaw and not feel like you are throwing the person on the other side out of their seat.

Looking at the balance and rhythm on a seesaw, we can understand better how our fluctuations are affecting others. When you are sitting on one of the extremes of a long plank balanced in the middle, there is not too much you can do. It is only when someone else sits on the other end that the magic starts. You are sitting on each end by choice. In the game, one person goes up as the other goes down. When you develop this back-and-forth or up-and-down movement you build a relationship. All based on having a central fulcrum, exactly in the middle. For every action, there is a reaction. The seesaw depends on an action to generate a reaction on the opposite side. Both people are part of the process. You both push up with your knees, to create the experience. In this process something repeatedly changes. One is up, one is down. There is a balance, an equivalent force. With a good rhythm both can connect. Did you ever, when you were a little kid and sat on a seesaw, have the naughty thought of pressing faster or pushing harder? What was the objective of that? Having fun or destabilizing the other? Do you see what happens in this playground of life? We move from one condition to another, creating comfortable or uncomfortable situations. Tilting the other is not fun. You end up losing their confidence and people will stop trusting you because your ups and downs don't consider or include the other. Why do people lose confidence and trust in you? This happens because they end up feeling they are abused, a punching bag. Being diagnosed does not give us permission to be that naughty kid in the playground.

To summarize before I continue with the flow of my story, check which setting your pot on the stove is. Is the dial set on high or low? See how high or low you are going on the swing. Look at how you are treating the other person on the seesaw. You know why this is important? Because if you keep hiding behind your armour, the one you have created to hide from others, you will end up alone, no matter how many people live or stay around you. This is the reality check we need to do today. Check how often you move from one extreme to the other. How this oscillation is hurting or enriching your relationships and how hard it is for you to live your life with no stimulus, with nothing external to keep you well: to be well balanced. All the things that make you fluctuate will end up messing you up. If you are low and use wine or drugs to balance yourself, you are lying to yourself. Those two, wine and drugs, will not ever bring you to your balance. Learn to live a simple and boring existence, for a while. Maybe in that silence, in that subtle yet real experience of being quiet where only you are the engine that sparks your life, you will find peace.

I went to see my psychiatrist and family doctor often and tried to keep a normal daily life. Even before the diagnosis, I was intense. I was loving. I was special with people. I always went over my own needs to fulfill and make the needs of others a priority. That was just me. What changed with the diagnosis? Well, my body was exhausted, and I started second-guessing myself all the time. The way people saw me changed because the diagnosis worries people. The people that love you want you to be okay and that is great, but then any change in your tone or when you raise your voice because you are exhausted, is blamed on the bipolar. Sadly, those moments of struggle, overpower the hundreds of amazing moments you had lived together.

At the end of each day, I rushed to clean up the house and be ready for the evening. It was a lived-in house, not a museum, so happy kids and a busy mom resulted in a quite messy house. A part of me knew that I had to stop the craziness and get the mess cleaned up so we could settle for the day. I was overwhelmed by ideas, playdates and activities in and out of the house. My kids had people coming over to play frequently, their moms stayed talking with me. They were so friendly and nice to be with. With the diagnosis, I became more and more sensitive to comments and much more defensive because I felt judged. If I rushed, or pushed for something to be done, it was the bipolar. If I was slow, it was the bipolar and my life got stuck in the significance of that term. BI-POLAR, two poles and never ever stable again.

The TRIPOLAR concept only came to me in May 2021. It was really the TRIPOD. The culminating moment of my journey, not of my illness but of the journey to be able to understand and come to terms with my own illness. For some time, I gave myself permission to curse, to cry, to fluctuate without constraint. I was not pleasant all the time, I have to be honest. But the more I let the anger and the grief come out, the easier it became to smile and joke about life. Yes, I actually made of my condition an act in the hilarious tragic comedy of my life. I drowned my tears and pain in optimism, and found the WHY and the mission. I became free to love and serve others, not focusing on receiving anything in return.

Honestly, learning to be on my own has brought quite a good number of blessings and a good amount of time to get to know myself, during good and bad days. The pandemic played a huge role in my current mindset. Little by little, life taught me how to slow down my mind. Stop and think before reacting. Newton's Third Law is formally stated as: for every action there is an equal and opposite reaction. That is physics. If you add emotions, the base of the human heart, it takes a bit of a twist: between every action and every reaction there is an emotional space. It is in that space that we find our peace and our happiness. Overreacting was always a trait, another characteristic of my TRIPOLAR mind. I did not know how to make that calmed space visible and accessible to me. I was always on the go-go-go. People got tired of seeing my activity pattern: one activity here, one activity there, always ready for the next one but never taking care of myself. I did not self-care because that was a word not known in my vocabulary. I was convinced I had to care for others and that was it. I never had time for a bubble bath or a date. That was part of the problem that made my foundation sink down. I was too much for too many, but too little for myself. I think I enjoyed living that busy life but, if you ask me today, I am not sure how much I regret that.

The part that I regret is that some people watched me and made the decision they didn't want to be like me. It was exhausting, and that is okay. Not everyone was able to keep my fast pace. I understood that people were different and that "being like me" turned for the better to "being with me." Amongst friends and family, I realized we all developed an independent identity. Sometimes I paid a very high price for my good intentions. It was during this time by myself, that wasn't really loneliness but my time of reflection and solitude, when I realized how toxic the go-go-go had been. I am still on the go more than anyone else. My friends joke saying they see my life, my trips, my projects in my social media posts, and it makes them tired. I know. I've finally come to terms with who I am, of what I want to make public and what I want to keep in my heart. I wasn't publishing my activities for others, or at least that is what I thought. I was posting things for myself, as a journal or daily record of the little steps I was making towards my recovery. This ideal was shattered when someone commented "What is wrong with her that she posts only skies and nature? Why is she posting all the time?" Well, I was appreciating nature as a gift from above. As I reflected on my own reality, every sunrise and every sunset gave a special meaning to my life.

It is our own experience with moods and feelings that determines our place in the mental health spectrum. We need to retrain our brains because they are fabulous. There are not mental health problems, but challenges that vary depending on your humanity and your emotional state. I am far more productive than many, more outgoing and I carry much more weight on my back than others. It's my reality and my choice. I could choose not to care and not to do, but that just would not be me. That would be someone else. When I embarked on this writing journey, I shared my vision with many, and I think I literally scared the heck out of them. It sounded crazy, and I knew it. I was trying to shed some light onto my own thinking, and many of the thoughts I had at that time are the basis, the structure of this book. Again, I had been too extra. My first draft of ideas looked already like a finished project and though rejection is hard to take, I understood that asking for feedback was a way of rerouting and polishing where I was going. It gave me the courage and determination to turn to writing not as a life raft in an effort to survive my midlife crisis, but instead turning these ideas into a self-refection that I could share with the world.

I am completely sure that I am a speckle of dust, a grain of sand in the desert, a drop of water in the ocean, yet I am looking for others who like me, in their insignificant and tiny little worlds, are willing to dream, reach out for their dreams and make a difference. But why? Because if this bipolar mind has hurt what I loved the most, there has to be a lesson. There has to be a way I can share, support and encourage others who like me have gone through love, hate and despair to find meaning in that struggle. I know so many valiant and amazing women living their own struggles and doing exactly what I did—sucking it in to continue on living a decent life. And, without being judgmental, because I know each journey is different, finding a purpose to our life in something that is not necessarily another human being.

This is where this bipolar gift needs to be unraveled. We need to support each other in our communities, in our mental health struggles going further, beyond words and talking about it. The talk is great, the conversations on mental health are fabulous and the way we see so many people struggling and talking about it is uplifting more than sad. It means we as bipolar people are also humans. We are not a different "species" we just have to work harder in understanding others and understanding ourselves. Mental health diagnoses scare the heck out of people. Here is where we have the golden opportunity to make a difference in life and in education.

Hasn't this pandemic hit us and twisted our paradigms upside down? It has. In the solitude or busyness or craziness or unsettledness of the lockdowns, especially the first one starting on March 12, 2020 when the world literally stopped in its tracks. We were made aware of the toxicity, carelessness and blindness of us as human beings. Our selfish ways, the way we affected others and how we were hurting the environment was made clear. The most selfish and self-centered society was put on hold by a virus and we lost what we loved the most—our freedom. We were a free society based on choice where the "I do what I want, when I want and how I want it" was the rule. Well, not anymore. Our comfy couch was turned upside down by the Covid19 pandemic, our ideals shifted. Survival, pain and sorrow was the new normal. How could this happen? Actually, I believe we had tested our limits way beyond what nature could handle and the virus stopped the harmful effects we were having on the environment in which we lived. The 21st century society was mainly greedy and proud, and that had to stop.

Looking back in time: the crazy commuting to work in the city, the way we perceived and talked about the people who worked in education, how we ignored the people who administered our basic needs, the massive lineups for concerts contrasted with the empty places of worship. The twist brought out by the declared COVID19 pandemic made first line workers heroes. Parents had to become teachers and educators. The streets were so empty, nature started to walk through those manmade paths, the people who we cared about had to be locked in and protected. Lots of lives were lost in the first months of this terrible time. It is impossible to know all the names, but possible to hold all of them in our hearts. Families separated, destroyed by pain and sorrow. Solidarity started to arise only to show how unprepared we were to care for one another when a catastrophe of this magnitude hit the whole world. Yes, there was also grace. The greatness of the human heart and the resilience and adaptability of the human brain started to put things together, trying to survive this challenge.

Part 2

I AM TRIPOLAR

DREAMLIKE JOURNEY

14
Breaking down Paradigms.

We all have a starting point, a turning point or an ending point in our lives. Life is just far away from static. We might feel proactive, efficient and really qualified for some things at some point and there comes the time we are not what we were before. We are clueless, lethargic, almost feeling useless. Our capacities change over time and more than a discouraging fact, we can see this as the great evolution of the human mind.

So many external factors, that were never noticed before the COVID19 pandemic have become so obvious. We miss getting together with people, at all levels, even with the people we don't like that much. Seeing our faces on the street, sitting or standing or lining up close to someone else has become uncomfortable. That sense of "my personal space" and "your personal space" has become more noticeable, at least for me. I have craved togetherness, but I've also craved isolation. We have learned to be there for one another, just in very different ways.

This pandemic has broken down, torn apart, destroyed many of the paradigms each of us had regarding life. It has also affirmed the need we have for one another, the way in which as a society we live, interact and care for one another. My hardest change, my challenge at the end of 2021 and moving into the first weeks of 2022, has been facing myself again in the mirror. I knew the last three years had been hard, and the last two of 2020 and 2021, have been the weirdest. It feels as if we were living in a different dimension, a multi-verse of our daily reality. The shock from 2019 and the effects in the world order when we added to our vocabulary the words COVID and pandemic will be felt for years, decades and generations to come. We are not an extinct race, we were in the process of extinguishing our essence by greed, carelessness and lack of concern for ourselves and the planet. We were a reckless society of consumerism and we still are. We have so many things we can get, we can dispose, and our life was something we took for granted. We mastered our days and nights until an invisible giant took on the stage where we were performing our lives and changed everything.

What we know today is that human beings are resilient and creative. We exceed our own expectations. We give value now more than we ever did before to the simple and the unseen. Those important workers who have been raised into the stars and yes, saved us from falling apart. I am not talking about the great leaders or the most seen or noticed. The ones that have raised up to the stars, and have kept our universe together are the doctors, nurses, dedicated professionals in all medical fields, and all the invisible people. The ones whose hidden work at stores, restaurants, mail offices, call centers, package delivery, cleaning services and repairs, were never acknowledged in their fundamental role in keeping society running together in synchronized harmony. We all have our own opinions and we have been prone to judge. No matter where we are at, whether we consider things are better or worse, we all lost something, but we also gained something we never knew we had. It was the ability to see ourselves and the world with very different eyes. I thought my mental health journey and my perspective on my own condition, as a bipolar patient was pretty much set. I did not expect big changes, because I, myself, was not making any big changes. I was pretty static. I had what I thought was a good balance of optimism and stamina, which is what I needed to be okay.

I had a really great learning that brought all these paradigms down and that is creating in me another sense of awareness. Realizing that my journey will never be over, not until the last day. We are so much more than what we feel or think, and it is so hard to see our own value. I discovered that other people see in me and believe in me in ways that, I don't even believe in myself. The world is rich not because of the money in it but because of the people that day-by-day touch our hearts, our souls and even those who at some point we believe hurt us. They all have a place in our story and in the person we are today. Life is a journey, and it is totally unexpected. We go through life making decisions with the information and knowledge we have at the moment. Call it resources, thoughts, feelings or needs. All these play a very important role to take us where we are heading or help us when we don't know where we are heading. This is the paradigm that I broke today. No matter how sure or insecure I am of where I am going, of what I am doing or what I have to go through there is always something bigger, someone bigger taking care of me.

I had a shocking experience in December of 2021. I had never participated in a Mission. We were going out into the streets, looking for homeless people, actually meeting them in person and listening to them. The mission prepared hot lasagna meals in aluminum foil containers, got fruits and drinks, that were packed in recyclable bags and put into backpacks. They also had clothing in ziploc bags. We went out by groups of 5 teenagers and one adult leader, driving our cars around the city of Hamilton looking for people in need. This was a Youth Mission, so I was acting as a parent volunteer bringing my kids and supervising, keeping an eye on them. I wasn't sure what we would find and I was a bit skeptical. In my narrow-minded head, it was the perfect way to do charity work, go drop and come back feeling great, because we did something for someone else. It turned out to be, for me, a wake-up call of my indifference, my hard but realistically, almost perfect life was put to the test again. I could not stop thinking of what had happened for weeks. Still, today as I write, I discover more and more the way this experience touched the delicate fibers of my soul.

We met at one of the Catholic Churches in Hamilton, an industrial city west of Toronto: a beautiful church and sacred space that, if you know me, I consider my place of refuge. This is the place where I find peace, where I recharge and leave all my stress, my failures, and my shortcomings knowing that God will bring something good out of my misery. Winter was starting and the temperatures had started to drop. We arrived at ten o'clock in the morning, attended mass and after a moment of silent prayer, we went down to the basement where we would be trained for the mission. We portioned the food in containers, packed it in recyclable bags and separated in three groups to go and look for those people who we could serve. I didn't know that the priests leading the Mission, had scouted the area in advance and had located the places where homeless people were living in tents.

COVID changed even the way in which homelessness was addressed. At this point in the pandemic, the homeless had been relocated to special areas, places where they could be "safer" in some way but also monitored by the authorities. I guess, trying to protect them from this infamous pandemic. If they wanted, the authorities could have made a census, counted them and found out the real demographics of these real people that live in constant need. I need a whole book to look at the humanistic vision of homelessness and poverty, not from the sense or point of view of capitalism and the way they are considered unproductive scoundrels but where we see them as valuable members of our society. It is more by fortune and mistakes that they have ended there, it is not by choice. I don't think people wake up one day and say, "I want to be homeless" or "I will do everything I can to end up alone on the streets with nothing more than a collection of scraps left by others in dumpsters and live like that until the end of my life, rain or shine." There are circumstances, decisions and actions that have led them there, not choices.

I believe there are so many things that happen in our lives that are circumstantial. They are not informed choices. They are the result of situations and actions taken by ourselves and others that re-route our lives in an uncertain direction. We can choose to buy clothes, a car, a house or groceries. We do not choose where we are born, who our parents, siblings and family members are. We choose what to study and where to live, but all these choices continue to be circumstantial and based on things happening which many times are out of our control. We don't choose the family we are born into, our siblings, our colleagues at work or our neighbours, who is driving or walking in front of us, beside us, behind us. We don't choose the people that are around us in a bar, a supermarket, a stadium, an airport, etc. And we can never predict or choose the people who are going to cross our path, at any point in our lives. We just live our lives as they unravel.

The same happens with mental illness and any other illness. We don't choose it, we don't get there, I mean, to become a patient of a certain discipline by choice as we all want to be healthy. The tricky part about mental illness is that we already have put in that word the connotations of "You are less." You are less valuable, less capable and less prone to succeed. When I went on that mission, I did not know that these real people had stories. I was not aware that they had lives just as complicated as mine, and that they were there, like all of us are in our own lives, due to decisions and circumstances. And no, I don't believe they are there by choice. They are heroes, hidden heroes in ragged clothes, living in tents set up in sandy parks and plain streets in the corners of our cities.

My bird's eye view of the day was clear, I could spot where we were preparing a group of twenty-five people to go on the streets. I could see the cars in the parking lot waiting for us to load their trunks with food, grab our team and get on the road to visit the selected locations. Scouting the area was really smart, because, trust me, searching for people in need, people that you can help is much harder than you think. Once we got in our own cars, we all set our GPS—Navigation System to the right address. GPS is the old term used when we started to track our trips with digital maps. We had a Whatsapp group to communicate with the group leader who shared their location so we could follow them to the first designated stop. We got there and wow, it was empty, no one needing help was there. From the time of the scouting three days before until that day, the people that had been living in tents at that specific park were gone. Tents, bikes, scraps, all they had was gone, and believe me, moving all that on foot must have been hard. We usually believe that homeless people don't have anything, because for us what they have might be nothing, well, for them that "nothing" is their whole world at that time.

This experience of meeting real people in unforeseen circumstances changed me. They were always there, on the streets. I didn't really see them as fellow human beings. They made me feel sad and sometimes scared. That was my bias. When the kids that were participating in the Youth Mission got out of the car, grabbed their backpacks and started moving into the park, I opened my eyes, wanting to make sure they were safe. I thought people could feel bothered, but I also realized they might need what the kids were bringing. What I saw from far away was the most humane and realistic interaction of two different worlds surrounded by grace. Pain was noticeable in the eyes of those people that the kids approached. The kids actually had to walk around and knock on their tents, telling them they were bringing some hot food and presents for them.

Not all the tents opened up to them. I know they reached out to a tent where John came out and he was with his girlfriend. He told them how he had been evicted from a building because he was bringing homeless people inside to feed them. Helping homeless people made him homeless. They told the kids many more details of their unbelievable lives. You could see, in their skin, the pass of time: the sunny days and the cold winters that had passed by. He even took the time to sing some native songs with the kids. I was touched by that simple yet profound interaction.

While the kids continued their conversation, a girl passed by. She was intrigued and hesitant and when someone offered her the hot meal, water, fruits and juice, she accepted it. There was a bit of indifference on her part. It was like an "okay, I will get it," and she kept walking until she got to a park bench really close to her tent. Her face was clean with quite a few band aids around her neck, covering scars she was recovering from. I could not understand the reason why such a beautiful girl would end down there under those circumstances. I got eager and walked to her fearing she would prefer to be alone. I asked her if I could give her some company. She did a shoulder gesture and I sat beside her. She said she appreciated the hot meal, most of the time, she said, people will bring a sandwich or something cold, this gesture surprised her.

I asked her name: Natasha, and she reminded me of so many girls I had seen growing up with my kids at school and in the activities they attended.

I assumed they all knew each other and to my surprise, the people in the different tents did not know each other at all, not even their names. That was an eye-opener. More than 10 people, each of them living side by side in different tents, on the same property were totally strangers. In my head, I remember each of the tents and they were all different sizes and covered with tarps. They were holding them to the ground with ropes and by placing around all kinds of recycled materials: from gas cylinders to tires, bike pieces, metal, and wood that kept the tarps tight to the floor, I guess to avoid water leakage. Inside there were plastic containers and luggage bags. It was incredible the things they had. It was not very different from what people prepare to go camping in the summer with their families. The huge difference was that what is fun and adventure for some of us, was crude reality for these people we had just met.

She continued to answer a few questions, while she ate part of that hot meal. She had asked for a second portion for her partner. While we sat together, she shared with me her age: twenty-four and how she had left high school. She lived with her mother until something happened, so she left, and she had not seen her mom in the last four years. Wow, she was a bit older than my kids and that burst my heart into tears. I asked her if there was anything special

I could do for her, and she asked me to pray for her family. That was a heart-breaking request. What a deep request because no matter how strained her relationship was or how far away she felt from her family, she still wanted the best for them. I asked her what she was doing, she said she was hoping for an opportunity, for something to help her out, but she just did not see a way out. I didn't really understand completely the kind of loneliness and despair she was feeling.

While I was immersed in my conversation with her, the kids were still listening to John's stories. One of the youth leaders kept playing the guitar, came close to us and asked her if there was anything she would like to hear. She did not know what to respond. Her partner came in, feeling a bit anxious about the people around the tent, invading his territory and circled around uneasy. We understood it was time to go. I saw her with my motherly eyes and told her, she was not the only one with a strangled family relationship. Some others were living with that same pain. I don't know if that made a difference to her or not, but it did to me. I never understood the pain of homelessness until that day. I had not seen what their life was like and what they had to face day after day. I had never been that close. We left the park and went back to the car as we had another place we were supposed to visit. A part of me stayed there looking at that young girl's eyes. In her sadness and pain, I saw the crude reality of life. Not everyone makes it in the same way, for some life becomes tough, with no hope but resignation. I did pray for her and her family for days. I prayed we might have the opportunity to meet again.

When we got in the car there was a silence, a type of awe mixed with disbelief, for the reality of life these people were facing and how unaware we were of what this mission was all about. It was about us learning from them and us meeting real people who were suffering. We were not there to feel good about ourselves. We were there to help others and share what we could, bringing comfort to them. It is unbelievable how this journey of life takes us to so many different walkways, with so many different ways of life. We drove to the third scouting station, and this was a bigger area with three groups of tents. It was a big park, three tents in a triangular shaded area under some big trees. Five more tents close to a wall, one beside the other completing that line of the perimeter and on the opposite side of the park two tents one big and one small, with a stroller and some children's toys outside. When our group went under the trees, we could hear a really strong discussion happening inside the tent closer to the road. That was a bit scary, the kids realized out of precaution, it was not a good idea to interrupt.

They moved to the tents beside the wall and went knocking or better said calling for people to come out. Out of the second tent, a couple came out, and thanked them for the hot meal and shared with the kids that they had just gotten engaged the night before. The lady inside showed the kids the ring with which her partner had proposed. It was a wow moment, where we realized there are many stories underlined under our own story. Some of the kids stayed talking, while the other half of the group moved on to tent four, as tent three did not answer back. A very young man with blue eyes like the sea came out and was shocked. He was actually the same age as the kids that were coming to disturb his peace. He was so grateful, his eyes teared up and showed the cleanness of his feelings. He said he could not believe that kids his age would come out to do this: that they would spend their time on a Saturday looking out for other people. Those eyes filled up with tears shined like crystals. I asked him, "What is the thing that you need the most right now?" and he said, "some love." His eyes and all of our eyes met. I asked if we could give him a hug and, in that moment, no matter any COVID protocols or any other regulations, we all moved close to him. It was probably the most felt hug I have experienced in a long time: sincere and painful. That is where all our tears started to flow. One of the leaders got all of us together and we prayed, "May God bring you peace, take care of you Conrad, and help you."

By the time we were leaving, two other people met us in the parking lot. They were riding bikes, their hands cold as ice, their faces flushed by the pedaling. The voices had spread around, and they asked if we were the ones giving out food. They asked if we had gloves and other things, and all that was left in the trunk of my car went on to them. The most bizarre thing happened. A not-that-old BMW stopped by us, and a guy came out of the passenger seat, dressed in ragged clothes, his face unshaved. He said he lived in another park and his friend had given him a ride to see if he could get some food from us. He received the leftover supplies we had, wrapped them around his arms, and got back into the BMW as fast as he came out. That was the end of the adventure of the Youth Mission that we did not understand completely when we started it. We went back to the church where there was a reflection time. We all left speechless, while we were going back to our normal and regular comfortable lives, reflecting on what we had seen, heard, felt, and how different life was for others.

It actually changed us. The way we felt about this experience, made us feel a bit uncomfortable, yet we understood it had been an opportunity to help. It was a reality shock more than a reality check. You can never compare circumstances or understand how life sometimes gets so difficult and messy for others. We did realize we were blessed by the experience and we knew we had to take that forward. A week later, there was another opportunity to bring Christmas Boxes to the same parish and share them with homeless people in the same area. I was naïve. I was way too optimistic. I saw this new visit as an opportunity, a way to see them again. We found some shoe boxes and we labeled them with their names. I went shopping at this place that opens seasonally and found lots of stuff at great prices. My family, my sister and her family, my friends, and the parents of the kids we went with the first time all pitched in to buy hygiene and self-care items, packed them in the shoe boxes and wrapped them in Christmas paper. The boxes filled with toiletries and goodies gave us a second opportunity, a Christmas miracle that really turned into a Christmas heartbreaking story.

A week later, we met at the same church, same drill, the difference was that it was a Family Mission this time so parents, children, and grandparents were organized in groups and had assigned areas to go to. We arrived with no plan. By coincidence we met the same kids that were with us on the previous Youth Mission, so we decided to get together in one car and drive to the same parks we had visited the previous week. We were told the tents were not there, but we did not believe them. We drove to the skate park, got out of the car and our eyes witnessed the devastation, some hardcore reality. Seven days ago, people lived there. The only thing we could see now were huge tire tracks coming diagonally from the street onto the grass. The area where the tents were standing was wiped off by a bulldozer and leveled to the point you could not even see any signs of what was standing there a week ago. A lady was sitting far away on a bench, watching her granddaughter in the swings, the park looked desolate, only another person walking a dog was part of that sad picture. I approached her and asked her if she lived close and if she knew what had happened with the people that were there a week ago. Her face showed sadness, her words were shocking, she said "something scary" had happened. A fire started on Wednesday night, and it consumed the tents. It seemed to be a candle that set one of the tents on fire, extending the fire to the others. The people inside had the chance to get out, they were not hurt. She also said it looked like the fire was manmade, on purpose, not an accident.

Our disbelief turned out into a deep unbelievable silence, "How could this happen?" In my heart, I remembered the kids talking with them, spending time together in conversation. The interaction of two extremely different worlds. I closed my eyes and remembered the kids doing the sign of the cross and praying with them. A question came to my head immediately, "God, how could this happen?" It was not only knowing we would probably never ever see these people again but our idealism was knocked over by blunt reality. Sometimes life sucks. That was not the worst part. After walking on the empty grounds, we decided to keep moving and drove to the other places we had visited, where Conrad, the newly engaged couple and the fighting couple were staying. We stopped in the parking lot where the two John's parked their bikes and where the BMW stopped a week ago, looking for some food and nourishment. It had been cleared out too. No tents or foreign articles, different from the playground structures and deep-rooted trees. We were devastated, we felt purposeless and almost hopeless.

We drove back to a huge area close to the shelters where people and some tents were set on a parking lot. This was a very different crowd. We could feel the commotion amongst the people in the streets coming out of the shelters and actually coming to us rapidly. They wanted the Christmas boxes. We gave them without realizing, some of them were getting double boxes. At the end, we could not even adjust completely with their reality. It was more the grief, the sorrow felt for the ones we had meet a week before, and it felt like giving a consolation prize. One of the ladies came stomping into the trunk of my car and started asking if I could give her almost everything I had in there. She literally said, "I don't have anything." She saw a bag, a luggage bag where I carried the PPE and the paperwork from some volunteer work we did on a weekly basis. I ended up emptying everything and giving her the bag plus some supplies like baby wipes and water bottles I had. Another of the adult leaders came close to me in disbelief, as she was asking and starting to grab more things. If I had something else useful, I would have handed it on to her. We closed the trunk because a cloud of people starting to move into that area looking for some more Christmas boxes, and we did not have any more left.

We went back with a flat-face and our minds puzzled, trying to figure out what had just happened. "How did that happen?" A day later, I was listening to the news in the radio, and they were talking about the shelters in that city. They said they had been filled up on the weekend, exceeding their capacity. That alone doesn't usually make the news because it was the end of November, winter was here un-officially and the cold days had started to hit. It was almost impossible to live outdoors and have an all-nighter out there, under those cold temperatures. That is why this reality does not make the news here, it's something we are used to, a shocking reality when temperatures go down.

They were talking about them because they had to separate the men from the women and assign the shelters by gender. The radio pointed out the disturbances and abuse that started to happen amongst couples inside the shelters, to the point the women had to be transferred to a different location. Men and women, homeless, had to be set apart. I am still trying to wrap my head around this double experience, its implications and its consequences. My tripolar mind wondered if the fire saved these people from a worse reality? Did this become their second opportunity in life? After all, some of them were together not by choice but because they met in those unfortunate and desperate circumstances. Maybe this was the way for them to get help, to bring back hope because God does not lose battles. God drowns evil in an abundance of good, I believe that. I believe that prayers change everything; they change our lives without noticing. We might not see the blessings at the moment, sometimes they really stay hidden for the longest time. For sure, in the long run, catastrophes, grief and sadness build us up, make us who we are and prepare us to live a different reality. Though my memory starts failing, I try to remind myself of these great, humble people I met one time. At the end we all matter, so I hope life brings us together again.

My life changed drastically in the following weeks. My mind was distracted and lost focus and unexpectedly went on strike. I was feeling an accumulation of stress and my body started acting out and overreacting. My clear mind, sensitive to all the experiences of the last weeks got burned out. Again, there was another twist in my life just before the Christmas season, that is supposed to be the most wonderful time of the year.

15

Living unproductive Overdrive.

Why am I writing this? That is a recurrent and constant question that goes through my mind, and I believe that I have so much inside of me that it actually handicaps me. I believe that if I can get all this out, what has been sitting inside of me for so long, I will be able to advance and move forward into the rest of my life. A friend that I appreciate deeply started reading the first part this book and shared a deep reflection. When her daughter saw the title of my book she asked: "Why would someone put herself out there like that?" What I understood is, why would someone write and explain so clearly their vulnerability? Well, I realized I have that same question inside of me. I just could not put it in words. Why would I put myself out like this? Will I regret it later?

Well, if I follow the same patterns of behaviour, my reactions and the cycles of my moods, I might regret it the day after I publish it.

I have to be ready for that, the fact that my own mind is my biggest handicap—never an enemy because you cannot live with an enemy so close to you. But it is in my determination to share my story, hoping families can get some light out of what this condition is, where I find my focus. I hope that people like me, who have managed their condition by shutting it down, see the value of their sacrifice. I have lived in a shell, hoping to keep my balance, by staying in a controlled reality, not wanting to see where loosing control would take me. I believe I lost a lot of creative power in my early years. I tried to use my energy on what I thought mattered at that time.

Now, I just have to put all that "smartness" contained inside of me into a much more productive life. I look forward to mornings where I can start my day with a goal in mind, the energy to make it a reality and the balanced mood that will help me get through it without losing my peace or being stressed. A day when one thing at a time is the essence of my being, not like now where fact, ideas, and thoughts mix together in an unclear and unhealthy manner. Where my attention span is focused and where my thoughts can be managed with the naturalness that only maturity and time give. This will come with time. The storm I am passing right now, another bipolar hit is being lived, documented in real time and will someday be a thing of the past. A building block for a better life where I can understand these deep thoughts inside my mind.

I have noticed this spike of the bipolar early. An over-reaction of my mind and it is unraveling in front of my eyes right now, as I write. My inquisitive mind is starting to differentiate facts from ideas and from thoughts. For many people, this might be the normal process in their minds, they do it effectively on a daily basis. They have a clear mind, a straight-forward path in thinking. Whether that skill is learned or imprinted intrinsically in your personality, you have a straight-forward train of thought. I don't follow that discipline. That is the cherry on top of the pie of my Tripolar mind. My mind goes down in circles and spirals, intertwining ideas. My mind is full of detours and forks and ends up being sometimes like a ride on an unpaved road. Sometimes it runs smooth, but sometimes it takes me to an unpaved road without really understanding where I am going. The truth is, that those who walk in the light, who have a clear path, understand there are many ways to get to the same place. You just need to know the destination. That is not the case for all of us. Where I am heading, that is very, very, very confusing at times. The path to get to that destination can be simple but for a mind like mine, full of forks and detours, it is hard to see the path, to narrow down ideas, because sometimes I don't really know where my thoughts are going.

We live in a world full of choices, depending on what we want to do and what we want to achieve. That path lays in front of you, and to access it you just need to understand one thing. You need to decide where you're going and how you want to get there. Do you want to get there now or do you want to take your time and enjoy the ride? Do you want to slow down, be an observer and enjoy your life? This means you have to avoid putting yourself in any situation that will make you lose your balance. Does that make sense? Well, I'm discovering that myself, in this self-discovery and self-reflective journey. What is easy and basic to many people, is not easy for me. I'm trying to put my thoughts and ideas together but I think that those ideas come into my mind and turn into thoughts that I cannot understand. If you ask me whether I can explain the things that go through my mind, I would say that I don't know. My great discovery in this new stage in my life is that there is a process inside my brain that I have to be aware of and they don't depend on me. They are just facts. For example today, it is raining, today is the coldest day, today is Christmas, or today is my birthday.

I am aware that when I am anxious, I eat anything and everything that is in my sight. I know I need to provide a safe space for my children to grow up. I have to pay my bills on my own. I know that life is uncertain. These are facts. There are things that need to happen and that will happen even if I don't want them to happen. I understand now that my hyperactive mind did not know how to project itself in the future. That my sensibility and attention to detail was affected by fear. That my creative and absolutely brilliant mind full of ideas, had been shut down by criticism. The eager and impulsive me, the one that went beyond what was in-front of me, the risk taker, had been slowed down by the consistent use of my medication. And that is okay. That is what turned impulse into reflection, reaction into a process of understanding and has sent me to the back seat so I can reflect objectively on what life has thrown at me.

Some people know nothing about this. For me, facts turn into preconceived ideas. I try to plan ahead, but I struggle to turn ideas into action because I have realized, my overwhelming and overreactive mind never stops. It is generating ideas constantly. I just think and talk, think and talk. When I am repeating things more than once it means my mind is in overdrive. I try to focus on the present moment, what I have to do. "I have to get ready. I have to go." Those are facts. "I need to get dressed and choose whatever I want to wear". Many of you can make choices really quickly. Choices are hard for me because I get confused when ideas build up one over the other. To focus my tripolar mind is challenging when I am off. When you drive, do you do it automatically? Yes, you are in the driving seat and you know when to turn. You just do it, automatically, checking your surroundings. When I am putting my head and my mood in alignment, sometimes I fail. My mood takes over and sets my mindset. It determines how I am going to feel during the day.

Let's reflect on the certainties in life, things I know need to happen. "I have to get ready to go and we need to eat breakfast. We have to leave soon because we're driving to Toronto and it takes at least one hour." Sticking to those facts is where I struggle because I have way too many ideas, more than I can ever accomplish. I thought I could meet some friends first, then go skating and walk with them downtown. So many ideas build up. I need to narrow down my ideas and make them so simple that I can act upon them. That is part of the awareness of having a tripolar mind. This awareness is helping me, and I hope can help many others to overcome any emotional challenges. I feel the anxiety in my body when I brush my teeth. I remember one of my first dentist appointments, eighteen years ago. My dentist said I had the gums of a fifty year old. I had very intense feelings, thoughts, and a lot of determination. Life was really busy, and I was adapting to a new country. Everything was new. I needed to learn and move forward, one step every day. I could tell that the intensity of my thoughts, was showing up forcefully in that simple task.

The force used to brush my teeth was as intense as the thoughts running in my mind. The same thing happened when I was writing. I could see the traces of every word carved in the next two to three pages. I guess that intensity of thought manifested physically in many more ways: in the way I walked fast, in the way I grab things, even in the intensity used hugging and greeting people. It was too much. I understand now why it drained my energy so badly and made me exhausted. After many years I broke down. Smiling to everyone and being positive on all circumstances was not sustainable. My investment in the outside world burned me so badly that I could not maintain that in my private, intimate world. There, I was blind, unloved and I crashed. I was lacking the unconditional love and commitment to myself, that would fill me emotionally.

My attention span right now is in overdrive. As you can see in what I am writing, I am piling up ideas, thoughts and reflections in an unconventional way. I am not following a straight line of thought but a squiggle of intertwining realities. I get confused many times by all that I do. I have to make lists and try to regroup. Editing this part of the book is a challenge, even to my Tripolar mind. I did a lot of dictation. Whether I was in the shower, cooking or getting set to go out, ideas came, and I was trying to record them in real time otherwise I would forget those wonderful sentences. These were pieces of my life-puzzle. I am always subjected to my emotions, whether I like it or not, that is a reality. This second part of the book was written in real time, as I was going through the ups and downs of an emotional breakdown. The consequences are more tangible, as they affected my day-to-day. My finances suffered. My fragility showed in the day-to-day activities that I could do and the ones that I could not do anymore. I hope sharing these struggles clarify my purpose. It is not fair to say that all those of us, who struggle with a mental health diagnosis, struggle in the same way. We all have a different emotional build up. That is an example of how our mind, our soul and our body determine the path we follow. I am trusting this process of discovery and I am fluctuating naturally. I hope as I continue writing, I understand better the place where I am at in this moment, with its joyful moments, struggles and sorrows.

I am coming to realize that I confuse ideas and thoughts with actions. It can happen to many people. We forget what we are doing, and our mind plays tricks on us and distracts us. That happens to all of us, at some point along the way, I know it is not just me. Do you have those times when we open a drawer, look at it and ask yourself, "What was I looking for?" only to turn around and go away because you can't remember what you were looking for? This time I had a paralyzed mind. My mind would not start. We had an important appointment today and when I woke up, it was too early, so I went back to bed for a couple of minutes, and that turned into one hour. When I woke up and started my day, I started writing what was on my mind for this book. I got in the shower slowly. I'm still getting ready but now it's late, almost time for that appointment. I have two hours to get there, only two hours. It's a one-hour drive, so I have to run now. I am getting anxious. We have no idea how traffic is going to be. Anything can happen, and we can't be late. Suddenly time starts either disappearing or the relativity of time takes over and time starts passing by so fast. Now breakfast is ruined. Who wants to eat in a rush? I had a picture in my mind, and I had the idea of making it neat, but now we're on the go. I didn't do what I had planned. I had to take a mental picture of my failings. My idea of making it a special day is now in the trash because we have to rush and leave now if we want to be on time. Yikes.

My emotionality is creeping inside of me, taking control over the reins of my personal life. I am aware I screwed up and have to stay in control of my emotional state. As fragile as it is, now I have to breathe, slow down my thoughts and hope it's going to be okay anyway. I am hyperventilating, so I do my bag breathing and count to ten.

I try to go back to the day I wrote these pages. In my mind I had images of the beautiful breakfast I was going to prepare and that haunts me. Oh well, it will happen another day when we have the time and are not rushing. This frustrates my mind and my soul and shows me the lack of discipline, and lack of fortitude because today my character is in the shingles, non-existent in the scope of thoughts. This plan will need to happen another day, so I don't get frustrated because it is very hard for me to let go especially when I attach my emotions to things. We had to eat fast and run out even faster because it all went wrong. The worst thing is I believe I did plan ahead. I did have a schedule in mind. We did have a plan, and I just didn't follow through with it. I got sidetracked and distracted, a courtesy of my tripolar mind. So, if you are like me in the tripolar multiverse of your own broken emotionality hear this: "you are not alone, you are not alone in this multiverse." I know many other people will wonder: how can this happen, especially those who are so accomplished and energetic, but it's not a bad or lazy disposition—maybe it is? It's just your energy is focused, mine is scattered, and it is not channeled in the right way.

A sequence of small actions leads our day-to-day. In my universe, I wake up, I put on my slippers. I stand up immediately, put my glasses on, and I have to plan and decide what I'm going to do. It is not coming naturally. I have to think and decide what I'm going to do next, struggling to focus my mind. I need to organize and sequence my thoughts to compensate for what I am lacking emotionally. I have to find the motivation to get ready and then determine when I am getting ready, I have to follow methodically a step-by-step method. When your mind is scattered or in overdrive, even the simplest task is complicated. What is simple: to prepare for a shower, take the shower, get out of the shower, put on my makeup and dress up. In the multiverse of my emotional fragility, this is absolutely heroic. Things go to another dimension and even the sequence is difficult to follow. I am forced to do the things that make a day. This is why many times when we are depressed, we can't even get out of bed. I am trying to describe that struggle as realistically as I can. When your mind is out of place, in overdrive, it is difficult to do things that seem really easy and straightforward.

I need to find a quiet space in my mind where everything happens with no drama. I need to be present one hundred percent, getting myself together to go outside because I am hardly making it on the inside. My hair looks curly, frizzy and messed up. I use this method in which I pin my hair around my head which keeps it straight overnight. We call it "la toga". You roll the hair around your head and secure it with bobby pins like a turban. This was actually the way people kept their hair straight before hair dryers existed. It works really well. I learned it in the eighties and it has stayed with me for over forty years. It makes my life easier, it saves a lot of time under the dryer, and my hair is sleek when I wake up in the morning. As I'm trying to put on make-up, my hands shake. Oh my gosh, I'm trying to do my eyes and I put the wrong shade, a yellow colour on my eyes, and I don't have time to fix it. I need to get in the car, I am super nervous, but "You fake it, 'til you make it. I know it's hard, but I can still make it." The truth is, I have to be okay, I am the backbone of my family.

I can see how my dispersed mind is reflected in my appearance. I've always worn earrings. I always wear them, and I never remove them. They are a part of me. I had never left the house without earrings and makeup. Now in my fragility, because I am so dispersed, more than ever I am doing things differently from how I've always done them. I am completely aloof, and I am embracing this reality without shame. Without the shame I am feeling for being impaired and going through this right now,

I realize what I have to do is acknowledge it and live with it. It needs a lot of acceptance, a lot of giving up on oneself, and accepting the fact that you are not at your best. You are not your own self. I learned to forgive myself for being so stupid and what I learned, is that doing stupid things is not done because you want to be stupid. I'm going out with no earrings, mixed makeup, and my clothes do not match. I am trying to get my sweater on and it looks weird and I don't care because today I am not having my head in a good place and no matter what, I am trying to be there on time. I will wear that anyway. I have to go out like this, and I'll come back to continue with all my random thoughts.

All of what is written in the previous paragraphs, happened in the intimacy of my mind, inside my head, away from my reality when being with other people. They might notice I am different, more drawn back, quiet, teary, or more laid back. This new experience is mine and only mine. Unexpectedly, I started seeing my whole life in slow motion. I have realized how handicapped I am from my own experiences. I did things in the past and the results were undesired and unexpected. Now I am realizing there is a Triple reality for me, A blurry trichotomy between facts, ideas and thoughts. How can this help anyone? Well certainly I have been lost, confused, wrapped up into the ideas of what my life should be, who I was supposed to be and what I was supposed to do.

I had an ideal of my role as a mother, wife and daughter. There was no blurry line to me between the roles, they were clear. When the emotions started to rule over my simple life, it started to get complicated. I realized that certain realities of my life were shut down. I was not aware of how people very close to me perceived my actions. I acted upon my thoughts, and I was quick, efficient and did a lot in a very short time. It took me years to detach myself from the idealisms. The dreams and hopes that I had, trying to be perfect. I had been trying to follow that path that I had set for myself since the beginning. Only after falling into this fragile emotional state, did I understand that I have been holding to the past, to those preconceived ideas too strongly for too long. This is the moment when I came to realize that what I have done for years does not work for me anymore. I need to make a change, an internal change that will lead my life into a new level of understanding. I have been sticking to my loses for too long, and that has made it impossible to open space for new things to come.

I see the many blessings and positive experiences I have lived in my life: immigrating to Canada and growing up in an amazing family in Colombia that valued what family is. My roles started to change as life started to unravel. Now I understand that I have to take the front seat of my own life and be the protagonist of my own story. I can't just be an observer of my life unraveling if I am to build my own future. Here is where I can start putting my fears aside and turn my experience into a wonderful opportunity of growth.

What I see right now, is that the confusion that I have lived in my mind in the past, a supposedly very bright mind, has turned me into an underachiever. Sometimes truth hurts but there is no way to hide it. Yes, I was idealistic. Yes, I was extremely positive. Yes, my life was based on ideals one after another. Trying to have a perfect life ran by the book, I came to realize I had actually messed up in life and missed opportunities. Giving of myself unconditionally turned out to be the best way to be undervalued and taken for granted, because I always thought more of the others rather than thinking of myself. Maybe this is where the fine line ends. At what point can I start doing things for myself rather than doing things for others? This is the process that I started by writing this book. Success, both in personal life and professionally, will always be based in the capacity you have to be someone and stick to yourself. I know where I am today, now, I have to decide what the next ten, twenty, thirty years will be. I am trying to find a balance, staying away from the regrets of the past because, whether I want it or not, the past cannot be changed. Where do I need to focus my mind? That is the real struggle for me in this fragile emotional state. Here is my TRIpolar dilemma: how do I check my reality and organize my thoughts so I capitalize on my ideas. A problem solver, a brainstormer, and a big mouth is just chaos when you don't have a clear path. My external mess is just a reflection of the internal chaos I am living right now. Practical and specific things turn out to be daunting for me because my head has lived for way too long between the slowdown of the medication and the paralyzing effect of my own judgement. I became handicapped because I considered that being bipolar was bad. That was a limiting belief.

Facts, ideas and thoughts are all over the place. That is where I am trying to get my thinking straight. Still bearing the weight of my emotionality in my day-to-day: waking up, getting ready, starting the day with a goal in mind, making meals, interacting with others, paying bills. All this is daunting. How is my mood today? Well, it is hard to tell. I do have an anxiety disorder, which shows up by eating to the extreme. I mix up foods and walk around the house, around and around with no clear actions. This sounds weird but yes, my mind generates an idea, and that idea becomes a thought, I elaborate, work on it, and develop it but the majority of the time, I never execute it. Why? Really . . . . Why? Because when the idea crossed my mind and I thought about it, the thought overpowers my will and triggers a dormant response which is totally dull. Thoughts blur my capacity to perform, and the thought takes the place of the reality. The result is a no-result: procrastination that is intrinsically related to trauma. The incapability to take action because the thought took the place of my will. It leads me to total inaction absolutely unmotivated to act despite knowing I have what it takes. It turns into an incapacity for doing things. I feel like one of those animals in a zoo, trapped in a made-up environment and just going in circles and circles around the small world set up for them by someone else. Believe it or not, that happens often. We feel trapped in our own reality. Some people experience it but they have a golden cage, a spacious and well-designed environment that allows them to thrive. I feel I am more in a small cage that is getting smaller and smaller by the day. Writing this now is a way of breaking out those bars that have detained me, trapped me in my insecurities and in my self-made limitations.

16

Tripolar Dichotomy.

In my condition, as a bipolar patient, I have realized there are two extremes. You either live life intensely and are faced with the aftermath or you draw yourself into this paralyzing effect of the mind. The in-between, is difficult to achieve. Why? Because after the first episodes I experienced, the confusion turned into caution and the caution into fear. None of this prevented falling again and again into the moods and the emotional swings brought out by simple things, like the weather. It has crossed my mind that if I had never left my beautiful home country of Colombia, none of this would have happened. Maybe I would have gotten the dream life, to be one more that lives her life as it was expected. Yet, it has been the adventure of my life to be able to see, two complimentary yet opposing worlds.

I embraced my loses. Can you win every single hand in a poker game? You can tell I am not a gambler. I have been too scared or prudent not to fall in behaviours that can lead to a path of addiction. I decided to walk the smoothest route, follow the path less traveled. This was my strategy, if ups and downs were hard, let's start keeping everything balanced, no matter how dull life could turn out to be. I made my choice.

We all have an irreplaceable role. We have an irreplaceable family. We need to understand how much we contribute to our family's atmosphere. We also have a huge responsibility to try to understand our own emotionality and to get through these dark times stronger and ready to keep up the unending battle with our own mind. Rather than the handicap word I used before; I would rather see this as a wonderful journey, discovering the depth of my own mind. I am not saying that other minds are shallow, many people have a more focused, simple and less confusing mind.

Every decision we make has consequences. Even the smallest choices change the course of our day and if you add them up, they change the course of our life. A good habit can be a saving board and consistency will give us the strength and courage that we lack. The hard thing is fighting against our vices. It is something that cannot be measured. You can end up being your worst advisor, deflecting from the greatness you are meant to achieve. I did choose the word "advisor" on purpose and would like to erase the concept of worst enemy because living with an enemy seems to be quite daunting. If you see yourself as an enemy, you start looking at yourself without the self-love and the self-respect you owe to yourself. The reality is you are really advising yourself. I have seen this in the last weeks when I realized that other people see in me things that I don't see in myself. The difference is that they live up to their value, raising high into the skies and achieving amazing things. Lives full of accomplishments. For me, it seemed to be something impossible to achieve or something that I would be unable to live. These limitations lived inside the mind. Waking up every day, looking at myself in the mirror and saying—I am the best, I am capable, I am a freaking badass woman, wakes you into reality and will turn your sleepiness into a wake-up call.

My dreamlike journey is everything but straight. It has been a rollercoaster of ups and downs, of discoveries but also of feeling lost way more than feeling right. I have kept writing, trying to organize ideas and thoughts, which are the two different realities I struggle with. An idea comes to my mind, but it is in that complex process of analysis inside my mind where I get burned out, drained and sometimes lost. I overthink.

When I thought my emotional journey was ending, that I had figured out my life and my future, I found myself in another maze which made me feel lost and somehow reckless. The pressure felt in my life with the new demands at work, in a world that has not yet been able to beat the

Covid19 pandemic, made me crumble. We all change. People change and as much as I thought I had always responded well to change; my mind was in one place and my emotional system was somewhere else. It all started with some crying. I knew it was time to apply those care strategies that I had mastered with age, self-knowledge and time. Far away was I from understanding the tricks that my mind would start playing. Under the circumstances of this pandemic, I did not expect work to be the same. Nothing was the same anymore. People come in and out of our lives. We are always looking for the best for our families, for ourselves and in this process, we got to interact with infinite types of people.

What happened to me was overwhelming and disheartening at the same time. No matter how much I tried I was not able to handle both physically and emotionally the changes that happen to me. I considered myself adaptable, flexible, easy going and always open to understanding others. That is what I thought, but the reality was far away from that. Why? I guess my mind was oversaturated, overpowered and overly concerned by things that ended up being out of my control, so I broke down.

In the last weeks of November 2021 I could not cope. I started crying and feeling overwhelmed in the middle of the day. I went in the morning to work and functioned well. I hit the job with more sensitivity than ever before because times like the ones that we are living in demanded of us more kindness, more understanding and certainly more concern. The why was absolutely clear for me at that time. These unprecedented times weren't easy for anybody. No one could be exempt from the challenges and uncertainties this pandemic had put on families, institutions and the core blocks of our society. All had changed and navigating the world was not a piece of cake anymore. By piece of cake, I mean not as sweet, comforting and enjoyable as they were before. Tough times for all. No matter where you lived or where you worked, we were all forced to change our ways. What worked in the past, well, it would not work anymore. Nothing was the same and we had to accept it.

We had to wake up earlier, be at our best, do self-screening before getting out of the house, check we were following public health measures to stay healthy and be safe for ourselves and for others. Things around me were causing internal reactions I was not aware off, triggering my emotional system into what I will call a fire alert. My conscious being spoken a language of calm. It's okay, you can deal with this. When I was with others, at work, in my social responsibilities, everything was all right. It all worked well. My emotional system started failing for holding in too much for too long and when I was by myself, I was emotionally fragile. I was concerned and wondered how much more I could handle and realized how all human beings are living in a different world. As long as our orbits don't interfere with one another, we will all keep well. Things really change if those orbits start to collide.

I felt sharp pains, excessive concern and deep emotionality. I started feeling I was walking on eggshells. All this put me in a fragile mental state. Not one that could change things, but one that would trigger feelings of fear, confusion panic and anxiety. I went to my doctor when my inside struggles turned into constant daily crying. I have always faced my anxieties and shortcomings with faith, strength and a lot of determination. Consistently, with my set of values, I have come through thick and thin in my family life and my relationships, trying to make decisions that I can live with. This hasn't always worked but I have been myself and have assumed the gains and losses of those situations I have lived in.

This new experience of extreme anxiety and attention deficit has been really tough to understand and even harder to deal with. I now understand many of the premises that I had applied with children who, at some point or another had been in contact with me. The sense of dispersion is overwhelming. I pick here and there, like a chicken in the ground. Starting something and leaving everything halfway is frustrating. I can't believe I had something in mind and twenty minutes later, after wondering around to seven different places I had not found what I was looking for. I could not even remember what I was looking for. My mind was aloof.

I am alternating activity with calm. I am not sleeping, at least not at the right time, but why? It is a vicious cycle of late nights or very early mornings. The question is always this: Am I ill because I am not sleeping or am I not sleeping because I am sick? The word illness has so many implications and I am using it here to show the reality of my emotional fragility and my mental distress. My mind was on strike, useless, like when you connect a battery to the opposing pole. No energy flows, it actually causes a short circuit that needs to be repaired, but how? Rest? Calm? Repair? Those don't work out that well for me. Resting makes me feel useless, calm gets me nervous and repair? Well, it comes from validation and affirmation. I read this in an Instagram post, "You cannot heal in the same environment that made you sick." This was an enlightening thought.

17

Breaking Down.

My mind is in an incapable state—and not a state of incapacity. The difference between these two terms is huge. I don't have the capability today to do things; I am incapable to move on. Incapacity refers to the guarantee that I would not have the capacity at all to be well. Asleep, that is where my mind wants to take me, it is 2:41 am, my eyes are finally closing, and my attention span is finally putting the guard down. Time to roll in my blanket and sleep. I have had three nights in a row like this. I thought that it was related to what I was eating before bed. In my anxious times I use food as a means of comfort and calm for my anxieties. On one of my worst days at the beginning of 2022, my son saw me eating and it was not funny. Now it sounds funny, at least for me, but his face was be a mixture of awe and disgust. I understand why, I was acting like a scavenger. I was just grabbing all I could see, serving it on a plate and putting it in my mouth, anxiously. I was filling my mind by having food in excess in my body. Here is where I can detect how my well-rounded and balanced personality, is affected by the emotional turmoil running inside of me. Again, you see me well, I look okay but I am not okay. A situation like this is absolutely unbearable for a deeply structured mind, even for a medially or unstructured mind. I was not acting by instinct to fill my physical hunger. I was following a desire to fill up a void. I wasn't even giving my body the chance to process one food after another, I was just on an eating rampage.

I HAVE TRIED TO GIVE IT A NAME, so when this condition arrives, I am prepared. I have seen it coming. This was a suggestion of my friend to start giving it a name different from my diagnosis, so by taking that name away I take away its power to overwhelm me and control me. At first, I was "Nahhh, that does not make sense," but it actually does, and I do not want to get any credit for that. This has been the strategy of an amazing woman who has learned on her own skin to deal with that ghost that is always part of our lives. Now I am thinking how will I name mine? The parrot, the monkey, the gorilla, or the elephant in the room. How do I want to acknowledge this reality that overcomes my being? For others it might be their saving board, their parachute, their karma. Yes, you can name it my static machine, my running track, my graceful tennis racket. You are able also to name it and rename it because you are the master of this creature, only knowable to you and created in the depths of your freaking amazingly, bipolar mind.

Can you imagine calling it as your favourite pets, Minty and Lola, or your first pets Goldy and Angelina, or your most loved ones Coal, Fluffy Ball, or your childhood ones Mac and Blacky, or the people you miss the most because you really did not understand at that time they stopped being a part of your life. Can you imagine how your perception of this hidden giant inside of you and me and everyone else changes when you relate it to something or someone? I can go on naming nasty or really fearful names, but I abstain myself of doing that by choice. They have come to my mind, and they even sound funny: the crooks, the witch, the badass, and I will stop here before getting into any disrespectful ones. Before I go down that path of recklessness and self-sabotage, I prefer to ignore them. I will not let my gift sabotage my mind.

Do you see how these last negative, unkind and pejorative phrases change us? If I am going to put a name to it, I am going to search it, research it, adopt it and give it the best name. I will pick for myself MY PARACHUTE. The one I need to carry with me when I am in my highs and the one that will slow down and save me from my falls, because my illness is up there in the sky, behind the clouds waiting for me to lower my guard and strike me. This is the power of my TRIpolar mind.

It won't be an animal that chases me or eats me up or an inanimate object that if I don't use it for its purpose would hurt me. No. My TRIpolar mind chooses the image that most likely will save me. So, if I see the signs starting to appear and I am getting anxious and feeling overwhelmed, I will get MY PARACHUTE and take control over it.

EVERYTHING IS ALREADY WRITTEN. This will be one more e-book, one more discourse, one more story to tell that has the immense value of a life given and a life taken away. It is nothing different from the reality of many who at some point have wanted to share their stories. I took this phrase from "A WOLF LIKE ME". Without wanting it to be out of context this is what season one episode showed in a casual conversation: " . . . you say you are trying to make everything perfect, but perfect doesn't exist. Perfect is the armour we wear to stop ourselves from being seen and maybe it is the thing that has been stopping your little girl from seeing you and feeling close to you. Maybe you should run towards imperfections, laugh and cry and dance, sing. Get messy. Messy is good. Break yourself open—it is how the light gets in". The main character says that, and she is trying to make the receptor sing to a child. She has created this fortress around herself. I feel touched by all these words. You are trying your best to be present, and she is pushing you away from yourself. WOW! This might be the next deep conversation I will have with myself. One I will have when I am better, and I feel better.

Another sleepless night and today is Blue Monday. YES, 1:25 am and I am still here, laying down in the living room. My sofa or futon open halfway, not flat. I have become quite attached to this couch that has become part of my days and my nights. I feel trapped in the bedsheets and the heavy weight of those blankets and covers in my bed. They make me feel I am asphyxiating. It is weird because the cycle of not being able to sleep comes with a repulsion for the space that we have assigned as our place of rest. I have ditched that space for three months, only using it when necessary. When I write, I start and end my day in the living room, in my lovely Structube compact sofa.

This sofa is in part the symbol of my new experiences, of accepting the changes that came into my life. I had to get something that served a purpose: to be the guestroom bed and that would also be the main sitting place in my tiny living room. This was a hard choice to make because we wanted it to be modern but not leather. It needed to be small to fit in between the hall and the wall, with no armrests to optimize space. It also needed to be comfy so we could all squeeze in and enjoy movies, games or whatever we decided to do in the living room. We made a great choice!

The so often called BLUES have come to me in rounds. They call them winter blues, baby blues or just to have the blues. What does that really mean? Informally, because they make this clear on my Google browser, they are "feelings of melancholy, sadness or depression." Another definition is:

> "For whatever reason, we all have felt sad or in other words, we've all been 'blue'. While it is common knowledge that it means feeling sad, sorrowed, depressed and a whole bunch of other gut-wrenching emotions, we've never questioned the association. Why would we use a colour to describe our feeling? So, what is it with the colour blue? Why is it associated with feeling sad?"

An interesting fact is, "Science Daily has a different theory altogether, based on recent scientific research. The research says—The associations we make between emotion and colour go beyond mere metaphor. The results of two studies indicate that feeling sadness may actually change how we perceive colour."

What you feel is in your mind. It is in your brain. You have to be ready to accept and dig deep into it. An Instagram post talks about the story of a boy with a broken mind. I believe we all have broken minds. Some might just find it easier to set goals, follow their dreams and fill in item by item in their bucket list. It is something about having dreams that empowers us. The condition of your mind, broken or not, might never change. It will be the way at which we look at it, how we feel about it and how we address our own understanding that will help us to move forward and relearn new patterns of behaviour to mold our emotional balance. I believe we all have a perfect mind and a perfect opportunity for it to be discovered.

I have learned three amazing things in my struggles to be a mom. Together we have had to fight three conditions that taught me how resilient, determined and focused I could be, yet I have not been able to do that with myself in respect to my own condition. The same has happened with my personal relationships. Why? Why am I able to be someone for them, for my siblings, nieces and nephews, parents, friends, colleagues and not for myself? Because I have not learned to love myself. I don't see myself in the way others see me. I am stuck in my own mundane existence, my own handicap, my own pity. I have lived attached to my limiting beliefs for a long time. Now I understand that my own resistance to change is recurrent. It is a way to hold me back and sabotage any good deed and advancement I have ever had. I am afraid of surpassing myself and not having an excuse for failure. I obsess over others and over things. I sit down to see others deal with life, experiences, and situations but stay locked in the carcass of my pride that does not let me move on, break the shell and take control of my own emotionality. This is not 100% voluntary, it is a 50-50 for me. 50% is self-perception and 50% is thinking about what others think of me. Being unsure of my self-worth.

Here is my theory. It is a mix of my experiences, my struggles and my shortcomings. I can make a list on one side of my talents and another of my shortcomings.

Let's do it in the four most important planes of human existence: the physical, social, emotional and spiritual realms. There is a need to take care of these four realms for a very strong reason. As I have learned from my child's scoliosis condition, we need to reach our sagittal balance. I had no clue what that was or what it implied, until I looked at the whole structure of our body. It was a foreign concept for me. My willingness to learn about this sagittal balance, what it implied and how to achieve it sent me on a learning journey. I had to study, learn, be prepared and have enough knowledge so I could understand. Learning about the sagittal balance in our bodies, took me on a journey of research and study. to deal with this challenge I had to reach a level of understanding I felt comfortable with and be the guide we needed as a family.

The same happens with my bipolar diagnosis. It is also the same that happens with anxiety, hearing loss, an expressive language disorder, parenting, housekeeping, education, and even legal information. I had to challenge myself to learn about it. Why is learning so important to me? Because I have to understand things first before I can start managing them appropriately. Because in my mind, when there is a problem, I have to find a solution. I am a problem-oriented person, prone to solve it, or maybe its backwards, I am a problem-prone person oriented to solve it. I don't know. One or the other the idea is the same. Tell me a problem, and I will try to find the best solution.

Here is where I am applying the limited learnings of my life to improve my future. We know what we know. We know what we don't know but we don't know what we don't know. We don't have a way to predict or anticipate the future. We don't have time travel powers to go back in time to change our mistakes or to go in the future to see the outcomes. If we had those powers, we would be so critical about our future. We would probably find a way to avoid pain and deviate from destiny. But our minds are far from perfect. They are the vehicles we need to step in, to get where we want to go. We only need to set a destination. It is surprising how life can pull us in so many different directions. Some of these situations are curve balls that we try to hit or to ditch. Here is where all life lessons take place. These experiences determine how we feel physically, emotionally, socially, and yes, spiritually, because no one can doubt we have a spirit, no matter how much we try to deny it.

Our bodies follow natural and rhythmical functions. They make us awake or cause us to fall asleep, sit or stand, or lay down. We have so many options, only limited by our physicality. We cannot fly like a bird, swim like a fish, jump like a monkey or glide like a swan. As living beings, we do have an instinct, yet we follow certain parameters of behaviour. We are capable of the best things but also of the worst things and last, we have to interact on this physical planet with billions of individuals just like us. I would not have had this perspective before the Covid19 pandemic. I had this intuitive idea of universality. I believe there is a greatness of the human mind but not to the extent to be able to form my own idea and theory of how mental health progresses and the challenges to make people more aware of it. This theory is valid for me, as no one else can base their learning on other people's struggles. I believe my struggles are a tool to untie, get unstuck and repossess my own understanding of my condition. The words redo, reunite, reveal, restart and recommend come to mind. I am writing as I figure out how this has been the process in my mind and how I need to follow my learning so I can be where I want to be. I know it will not be a smooth journey because more curveballs will keep coming my way. These kinds of balls never stop coming at me. Life is unpredictable but they are preparing me to live a life fully aware of my potential.

I don't know if naming that place would empower me or affect me. Here is an exercise: I am bipolar. Is that a limiting belief or an empowering belief? Is it limiting me by the fact that I like to call myself TRIpolar? Am I depressed now? I know I had panic attacks and that I felt paralyzed by fear. Are those words the reality of my life today? Are they limiting me or empowering me? Have they made me emotionally fragile? I cannot ignore the fact that those four descriptors: bipolar, depressed, panic attacks and paralyzed by fear are feelings that are present in my life today and they determine the state of my mind. That is a FACT. Then come the ideas that rumble inside my head, first weighting me down, as if I was carrying a ton of rocks on my back. They rumble in my head, confusing my being, blurring up my perception of things and messing up my emotionality. These unconscious ideas come to my mind in the same way that dust accumulates over any object that has been kept static. I don't know how these tiny speckles of dust accumulate. I don't know how they start getting in my head, out of nowhere, covering my brain with overwhelming thoughts. But there is hope. There are also bright speckles, like sparkles that make my brain rise and see things with that brightness. These thoughts are the glitter in my life. Both dust and glitter live inside of me. How do I determine which will stay and which will go? Which ones should I embrace, and which ones should I discard? They both grow like spider webs and if I don't remain watchful of those thoughts, they continue growing tightly intertwined, as a real spider web. They are catching up my dreams and hopes and wrapping them until the hopes and dreams are suffocated taking my life away and killing them.

Those cobwebs in my mind limit and make me so vulnerable that I can be eaten as prey. They take away my happiness, my reality, and my strength. Do you want to know why? Because in one way or another, I allow it. I have seen the cobwebs or the spider webs forming in my head. I know they are there because I see them. I can feel them enclosing me mentally and paralyzing me physically. Have you ever brought down a spider web with your hands? They are gross and stick to you in a way you can't just get rid of them. They trap your skin and have such an immeasurable force that you need some extra power—probably you will need to use your other hand to remove it, in a messy and quite disgusting way. This is what happens with this overwhelming flow of ideas, dust or glitter. They end up covering you, making it a perfect setting for the scattered brain to come, shoot its webs and trap in the good and the bad inside your head. This clouds my judgement, making me foggy, and ends up laying the brain into a state of disuse and neglect that alters my balance.

I am not sure if I have it clear. Facts are dust and glitter, and ideas are spider webs. We don't control the dust and glitter coming to our lives. We somehow can only control partially their intensity, by the way we react to the dust or the glitter falling over us. Too much glitter is mania. Too much dust is depression. The cobwebs come into place, fogging our perception and feelings of overwhelm, insufficiency wrapping us up. How does that happen? It happens unexpectedly and very quickly when we are not looking. The spider comes out to build its web even if we are fully aware of its presence. It does it while we sleep or while we are distracted, and it has its own rhythm and power. You cannot kill the spider making your cobwebs, because it hides in the deepest part of your brain. We can see the webs forming those symmetrical patterns that make them unpleasant, but we are unable to just cross through them. These patterns have a life of their own. They are elastic, malleable, and made to trap you inside. Once you are stuck in them, the spider comes quietly, stealthily and weaves you in.

My book is being written as it comes out of my mind. Those last paragraphs are intense and sound really crazy to me. I can tell emotionally where I am standing. I am on a bad day. Looking at it now, I am starting to understand the complexity of my thought process of analyzing facts and lived experiences; separating them from positive and negative ideas and then moving onto conscious acts I can control turning them into thoughtful actions. I am finally finding a space of peace between the stimuli and the response. I can think through things and manage my response—not control it yet, but it's getting better. I am having a total awareness of facts, circumstances, environment and ideas. I am processing information following this method. I can now understand that I can be feeling calmed, overwhelmed, joyful, empowered or drained. Millions of emotions can refer to these ideas in my head without letting myself be dominated by them. My emotions reflect on ideas that are created unconsciously in my mind, tasks like stand up, eat now, drop that, go to sleep. Positive and negative, dust or glitter.

Being thoughtful of how our actions affect our moods requires training, perception and knowledge at the service of your mind, and yes, I forgot the most valuable, experience. These are four characteristics of the human mind that come into play and help us have a clear train of thought. No two individuals use or have the same logic. Logic is the sequence of thoughts happening in your mind. They are subjected to our life experiences, the training we received, the way our senses perceive the world and the knowledge we have. Knowledge in this case can be seen as the software with which our brain operates. We have a lot of similarities to and a lot of differences from computers and how they work. They are just irrational. The biggest difference is we are alive. We make choices and computers don't. They remain dormant until we activate them. Then they can work for a finite period of time, just like us because we both will die one day. A new computer can die of a system crash, and we can die in an accident. We can harm our computer with a virus, as our bodies can be harmed by many viruses, some known and some unknown—think about this pandemic. We've had to recur to vaccinations to stay safe, and computers need antiviruses created by men, to correct what was damaged by a virus. Sometimes they work, sometimes they don't, and you lose everything.

We have a hardware—our bodies- and a software—our minds. We have a spirit that adds feelings and conscience to all our actions and no computer so far has been able to mimic that. Computers can perform tasks and operations better than us, to the point a good robot can replace the work of hundreds of people doing things manually with an almost inexistent rate of failure. That is the process of industrialization, born of ideas, turned into thoughts, developed in the human mind and made real by human hands. A robot has been designed, assembled and repaired always by human hands. There is no doubt the world needs us. Even with the most advanced cars and medical equipment, they are not performing tasks at their own will and initiative. Every machine needs to be turned ON and requires some kind of energy to function.

We are the most amazing machine ever created. We come to existence through a process totally independent from us. We don't choose to live, we just do. We are also the conductors to make life. Yes, love is the conduct to start a new life. I know this is a tricky subject emotionally, and if we look at science only, we can abstain from bringing that emotionality into this reflection. We need an ovule and a spermatozoon to join up under certain conditions, we can't control. It is not like making scrambled eggs where we crack the shell, get a yolk and egg whites, scramble them and voila, a delicious breakfast is done. For a child to be born we need both the male and female parts. We all are the result of a male-female interaction under certain conditions–not always positive sadly, ending in a new life being created. And life can only grow under certain conditions. No matter how much technology advances, we can't make a baby in a test tube. It needs a womb to develop. The womb is a part of someone's body. It is the receptacle of the miracle and becomes the feeder, the bearer of an energy so intense and so profound that a gamete turns into a child.

We give different names to the evolution of man. In very basic terms, from a pregnancy we can expect a baby. Two cells become a fetus that grows and develops with the most incredible biomechanical, neurological and physical qualities that one day, comes out of the mother's womb. Inside the mother's womb is where life forms from the beginning. Only life sets all the processes on. We cannot deny the existence of electricity. We might not see it, but we know it exists because it has physical changes, advancements and circulates out of our own will or desire.

We can speculate and try to manipulate the process of giving life, but no one owns it. Life starts and keeps growing. No matter how much we want to control this process, we can't select the physical characteristics or even predict the features of the face and body when someone is born. We will never know how a baby will look at birth. This will always be a surprise. We can't know how they are going to look as they grow, how tall they will be, what kind of hair they will have, or how they will talk. The eyes, skin, hair, and all physiognomy are a mystery. We don't know how tall we are going to grow and until what age. We don't know how we are going to age, and we definitely never know when we are going to die. As human beings we want certain things, but we can't control everything.

We have three things: conscience, will and intellect. We know right from wrong. It is imprinted in us. It is more than just an instinct, a sixth sense. The purpose of living seems to be to avoid pain and pursue happiness. We all want what is best: to have enough food, clothing, and shelter, to be healthy and happy. Conscience is that inner voice that judges our actions and lets us know if what we are doing is okay or not. Our actions become a virtue or a vice. My conscience leads me to act in one way or another. Conscience for me is an internal process of understanding, something between me and God. No one else can determine our conscience. We can differentiate right from wrong naturally and that perception leads our lives. Our actions are decisions made by our own will following our moral compass. "What is right is right, even if nobody is doing it. What is wrong is wrong even if everybody does it." This is a premise I learned long time ago, which formed the base from which I will explain the importance of how we manage our thoughts.

Ideas flow millions in a millionth of a second. Our brains are amazing and if you have been like me, diagnosed with a mental illness, it only means you are officially recognized as amazing, because even if we understand the regular standards of norms in our society, they have not yet understood our grace and our power. So, please stop calling us mentally ill. It's annoying being analyzed by fellow human beings trying to fix us. They are trying to put us into a mold, depressed, anxious, ADD, ADHD, bipolar, and so many more terms. I get it, we need to give our physical, spiritual, social and emotional conditions a name. I am grateful for all the people over centuries that have contributed to the advances in science, medicine and technology, that help us to be where we are today. You are real heroes, especially the ones we don't know about that worked with the geniuses that got the credit for it. The truth is that they would have never made it on their own, without the fellowship of other humans that acted upon their discoveries. In a chess game, you would never win if you didn't use your pawns wisely. Some people are the head, some people are the hands and some are the feet. Some have the ideas, and some make their ideas a reality while some transmit them so we all can have what we have today. An advanced world built over centuries, millions of years, one stumbling block after the other.

Will is the capacity I have to decide upon one thing or another. In general, decisions have two sides: we would rather do it and follow the consequences or we don't do it and still follow the consequences. The way in which we follow is determined by many factors, mainly our physical, emotional, social and spiritual being. But in reality, that is what we carry on our backs and is what we have in our backpack to follow whatever path is revealed to us because of our decisions. It is a cause-and-effect relation. We have to understand the importance of our will, especially when we are emotionally fragile, because that emotional fragility caused by physical changes challenges our perceptions.

As a bipolar patient, I have an imbalance in my brain that is both chemical and physical, set on by my biology. My biology is my age, my gender and my body functions. These body functions, as with any other living organism, are foreign to us. I don't know how my digestive system is working, why I feel hungry, thirsty, tired, happy, or energetic and how my system pumps blood to my brain and to every limb of my body. Every organ acts in a perfect balance, making me and my body stay alive. The chemical balance or imbalance is so very sensitive. I can be mechanically well balanced, chemically well balanced or biologically well balanced. It is in the biomechanics of our body and in the chemical structure that is feeding my body and my brain where I can excel or be torn down.

Sometimes our physicality represents limitations and emotions shorten up or fire up our capacity to react, but it is in the chemical component of our brain that we reach our full potential. Not everybody will have the same potential. We all are made to be great. Our greatness is not in how we feel, look, or present ourselves. Trust me, emotional fragility is many times a self-sabotage of our minds trying to hinder us and make us fall. Emotional fragility starts with a chemical imbalance, caused by physical changes in our bodies: excess production of something or a lesser amount of something else. Whatever it is: lack of protein, excess fat, lack of water, or an excess or deficiency of sugar, all that we put in our body affects us in a positive or not so positive way. We fail by excess or deficiency because, contrary to what some would think, balance is acquired by checking on our extremes. We can be extremely careless or extremely cautious.

My undiagnosed hyperactivity is shown by excess distractions both in mind and body. I plan activities for myself and others and never finish them, I leave them incomplete. It contrasts with being extremely positive, enthusiastic, outgoing, while fighting every obstacle with a smile. I consider this to be my journey of constant put downs and discouragement. I always was prone to action, then I noticed the signs of my mental confusion. It shows in how organized or disorganized I was at home. I have more things than I can manage. For years I have been criticized into throwing out all that useless stuff but . . . but . . . It has a meaning for me. Yes, many times I have more than I need, especially in the craft area. I also have duplicates of many things, from pieces of clothing to gifts. I simply cannot buy just one. My mind unconsciously grabs, pays and packs a few more just in case. You can't imagine how many times I have done an in-person or online purchase that I regret immediately. I am not sure it is attention deficit or hyperactivity, or simply another trait of my TRIpolar mind.

18

From Bipolar to a normal Mind.

This is a letter from me to me, to the one you call Bipolar.

"I am just like you; you are like me but many call you normal. We are made of the same fabric, and the same feelings and thoughts run down our brains. We are not twins, not even a mirror image or a shadow of each other, we are just the same. My normal me and my bipolar me are just the same person. Sometimes they feel like strangers, like they were two different realities, even incarnating two different bodies, but that cannot be true. I have to say this to you. If my bipolar mind was to be a stranger, someone away from me, it would be two different bodies, as the tattoo on my arm: "Two bodies, one heart."

My bipolar is the opposite. "One body trapping two hearts." It really feels like my bipolar is two minds budding. It is like having to live with two different hearts. If I had a twin, we would be practically identical bodies, two hearts and two minds beating at a similar rhythm. There is a connection built by birth, and that no one nor science can explain. It is not a perfect simile or example, because both of our dear bipolar and normal minds are difficult to understand.

If it was to be a reflection of me, that I believe would be the best way to explain, it would be same heart and same body and same mind. That reflection is the transposing image of my own being. There is no magic trick. You can see your image reflected in a window, a glass door, your car, or a mirror. You can see different distortions of the same image if the mirror is concave or convex, or if it has a certain difference in perception. This is why many of us need glasses, because we need to correct that distorted image we see. Whether the image is blurry or clear in the vertical or the horizontal plain, we try to fix it with a visit to an optometrist.

My bipolar mind and my normal mind are a two in one. I have only one body, working together to keep me alive and running. I have one heart to love myself, my life and the people around me. I have only one mind to figure out where I messed up. Where did I miss the mark, lose myself and end up feeling lost? That was really an idea in my mind. Now with my conscience and will, I will make this statement right. Here it goes:

> My bipolar mind and my normal mind are ONLY one. I love my body, and both MY BODY and MIND are working together to keep me alive and running. I have one BIG and EXPANDING heart to love myself, my life and the people around me. IT IS THE WHOLE OF ME that tries to figure out where I messed up. THAT IS A REALITY: WE ALL MESS UP. How can I continue working with mind and body to keep loving myself and others to reach my full potential? None of this is possible, if I don't care for my physical, emotional, social and spiritual being. We are here to help one another.

Yes, those are the ideas in my brain being thought out. I have to remove that part of me that without even noticing, sabotages all that I do and that turns all of my good actions and intentions into regrets and makes me second guess everything that I do.

It's exactly that little angel and that little devil we see in the Disney movies, interacting in a constant fight. At some point, I have to put them both to sleep and THOUGHTFULLY follow my newly discovered mind, the one that is not either white or black, cold or hot, up or down. I have to THOUGHTFULLY USE MY TRIPOLAR MIND, the one that optimistically sees the colours in everything. When the dark times come, this mind can differentiate in what part of the gray scale I am and show me how to act and react to get myself in that delicate and hard to achieve balance of my emotions.

You are never going to be accepted and loved by everyone. Some people will hurt you and don't really care. You are going to be loved and hated, wanted and ignored, because the opposite of love is not hate, it is indifference. That is worse than hate, because if someone hates you, at least they still feel something for you. But when they are indifferent to you, they don't care and they will never acknowledge your pain or apologize. They will never open the doors to you so you will be able to apologize. You might never hear the words, "Sorry, I didn't mean to hurt you." Someone's silence might mean "Well, I am not sorry, I don't give a shit." or even, "Why should I be sorry?" These are very different ways to use the word sorry.

On Instagram I saw a post making this question, "Do we really need it?" Do we need an apology? Because as Sandra Bullock put it in an interview: "Not everyone that hurt you cares." Keep discovering yourself, accept who you are and start thriving!! I will end by saying I am sorry if what is written in this book doesn't apply to you, please learn about it because maybe one day with these ideas, you can help others.

I am also sorry if people don't understand your mind. I hope these thoughts, ideas, feelings and reflections somehow enlighten your journey. I am sorry, not everyone is going to like this, but you have to do what you have to do. My last sorry would be "Sorry if I ever offended you, trespassed any boundaries, lacked understanding or stopped looking at you with love." Sometimes life is like that. I would like to say it is not our fault, but the truth is, whether we want it or not, everything that happens in our lives is our fault. We need to come into that realization by ourselves and not blaming others to justify our decisions. I hope we can realize one day that we need to gain our emotional balance because if we are not happy, it is our own fault.

Epilogue
The Work of a Lifetime.

My life experience, the things that have led me to where I am today, are the result of three lockdowns. Yes, both 2020 and 2021 have been years of great uncertainty, deep sorrow and have been tumultuously an accumulation of misfortunes. All the tragedies that we have lived, big and small, that have generated movements around the world that look for justice, inclusion, respect and reconciliation, have touched our hearts in deep ways. No matter how difficult it has been, how sad these tragedies have been, the world keeps turning and turning, waking us up to a new day, sending us to sleep with a new night.

I hope that this book, becomes what it is meant it to be: a self-discovery and a self-reflection for anyone who reads it. I don't know you, and I hope you are not disappointed coming this far. If I know you, I am very lucky. You have the last word because what I am trying to do here is use my fifteen minutes of grace–that a friend once assured me we all have in our lifetime–to share my knowledge and experiences.

I am taking a leap of faith. I really want to be able to get this book out to prove to myself that I can really do it. Then I want to work for hours so that, one day, I will have enough time to choose. To choose to go out with my kids on vacation, to visit my parents, to uplift the people I love. I dream of giving other women the opportunities that I wish I had while I raised my kids. I saw them wake up, go to school and play with friends. Our family ate together and went on vacations. We even bred puppies, seven puppies born in our home, from two different litters. All this was possible because we cared for each other.

The good is all in here, I mean in my heart. The bad has been a learned lesson. The not so bad is what made this book possible. I dream of women being able to be productive and happy while raising a family because no matter what the outcome is, marriage is worth it. If you have loved deeply, and have been absolutely in love at least once, the end is not what matters. It is the road you walked. I have lived a great life. And the part that made me courageous and hyper-active and hyper-productive has helped me to be at peace, as I have lived my life with intensity.

Please appreciate your journey and love those who are around you for who they are. Don't try to change them because they are around you for a reason. Don't send them away thinking that separation and divorce is the solution. Make it work if you can because a whole person needs others around. If you have a chance to love twice, do it, no matter the circumstance. I know it feels great, but never make your happiness the unhappiness of another person. That is not what we are here for. Be brave, be bold and live with integrity. Being alone is impossible because actually, we are never alone. God, Our Father and Our Creator is always here, seeing us grow. He put you here, in this time and age for a reason and He wants to see you happy and fulfilled. Life is worth it, even if you suffer because in the middle of suffering, we discover ourselves and find redemption.

I am not the only Bipolar person in the world. I AM TRIPOLAR and there are many more like me: FUNCTIONAL and SMART. If we join efforts, we can make this world a better place. We can beat the stigma of bipolarity together.

My wish for you is to live long and love deeply. Discover the magical gift that only you have and learn. Try out new things that help you grow and avoid anything that can hurt you both physically and emotionally. Because at the end of your journey, you will have the chance to name your story.

My story has been named "I am not bipolar. I am TRIPOLAR". I hope you take something from my story and one day, you can write your own.

UPCOMING BOOKS:

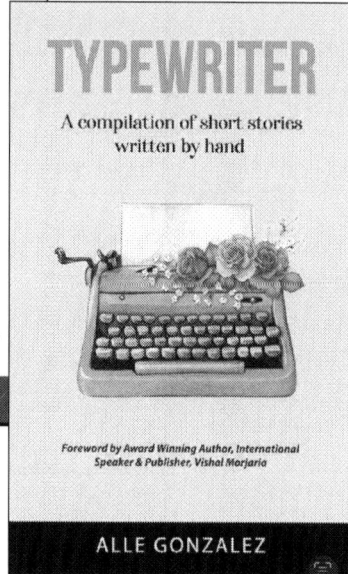

NOT an ECE

The principle-based guide to become your child's best Childhood Educator

Foreword by Award Winning Author, International Speaker & Publisher, Vishal Morjaria

ALLE GONZALEZ

TYPEWRITER

A compilation of short stories written by hand

Foreword by Award Winning Author, International Speaker & Publisher, Vishal Morjaria

ALLE GONZALEZ

TO FIND EVERYTHING
ABOUT BEING TRIPOLAR
CHECK MY BLOG: